WAR SO TERRIBLE

A Popular History
of the Battle Of Fredericksburg

By Donald C. Pfanz

Page One History Publications
Richmond, Virginia

A Page One History Publication

Copyright 2003 by Page One Inc., publisher,
PO Box 4232, Richmond, Virginia 23220-4232

First Edition

The text follows closely a series of articles written by Donald C. Pfanz and first published by the Fredericksburg *Free Lance-Star* in 2001. The illustrations were gathered by the author from many sources; a list is published on page 120.

Book design and map design by Norma Pierce.
Printed by Worth Higgins and Associates in Richmond, Virginia.

ISBN 0-9704367-1-8

*"It is well that war is so terrible;
or we would grow too fond of it."*

— Robert E. Lee at the Battle of Fredericksburg

To my wife, Betty

The author gratefully acknowledges the cooperation of the Fredericksburg *Free Lance-Star* in the preparation of this book. For additional information about Fredericksburg's Civil War heritage, see the *Free Lance-Star* Web site at www.fredericksburg.com.

Contents

Introduction

The following articles appeared as a series in the "Town and County" section of the Fredericksburg *Free Lance-Star* between the months of January and October 2001. Written in a casual style and focusing on the human drama rather than on strategy and tactics, the articles are designed to appeal to Civil War buffs and novices alike. Much of the material quoted in these pages comes from original manuscripts and is published here for the first time. Because the series was originally written for publication in a newspaper, no references are cited.

Many sites mentioned in this book are readily recognizable today. Others are gone, but their sites can be found by their proximity to modern landmarks. When possible, I have tried to tie historical events to existing features. These features will not mean much to those unfamiliar with the Fredericksburg area, but I have let them stand as they provide handy references to anyone wishing to tour the battlefield.

My goal in writing these articles was to inspire Fredericksburg citizens to learn more about the Civil War history of their area. For several years the Central Virginia Battlefields Trust (CVBT) has been striving to save battlefields near the town from destruction. Sadly, at Fredericksburg itself there is little left to save. The plain fronting Marye's Heights, on which thousands of Union soldiers were killed or wounded on Dec. 13, 1862, gave way to residential development early in the 20th century, decades before the battlefield became a national park. Light industry and residential development threaten to devour what little historic land remains.

The picture is not all gloomy, however. In 1998 the National Park Service, with assistance from the CVBT, acquired a key parcel of land on Marye's Heights. Another victory came in 2001 when the Fredericksburg City Council agreed to give up the city's right-of-way on the Sunken Road. As a result of its action, the National Park Service will be able to close the road to traffic and restore the road to something resembling its Civil War appearance.

Successes like these are few and far between, however. Throughout America, Civil War battlefields are vanishing at an alarming rate. The federal government cannot, or will not, commit the funds necessary to save these lands. If they are to be preserved for future generations, private citizens must take the lead. Several grassroots organizations are working valiantly toward that end. The Civil War Preservation Trust (www.civilwar.org), the Central Virginia Battlefield Trust (www.cvbt.org), and Richmond Battlefields Association (www.saverichmondbattlefields.org) all do excellent work. Please give them your support.

Several people have assisted me in the preparation of this book. In particular, I wish to thank editor Gwen Woolf and publisher Joe Rowe of the Fredericksburg *Free Lance-Star*. Both were highly supportive of the newspaper series, and they have been no less supportive of my efforts to turn the articles into a book. For years the *Free Lance-Star* has been a leading advocate of preservation in the Fredericksburg community. In recognition of its efforts, the first $1,000 from sales of this book will be donated in the newspaper's name toward Civil War preservation.

The writing of *War So Terrible* would not have been possible without the help of my colleagues, past and present, at Fredericksburg and Spotsylvania National Military Park. Their diligence in acquiring manuscript material on the battle provided much of the grist for this book; in addition, several members of the staff read the articles prior to their publication and offered suggestions for improvement. The series benefited as a result of their comments.

I also wish to thank Don and Norma Pierce of Page One History Publications for their efforts in publishing this book and my wife, Betty, for her love and support.

— Donald C. Pfanz

The Armies March to Fredericksburg, Nov. 15–Dec. 5

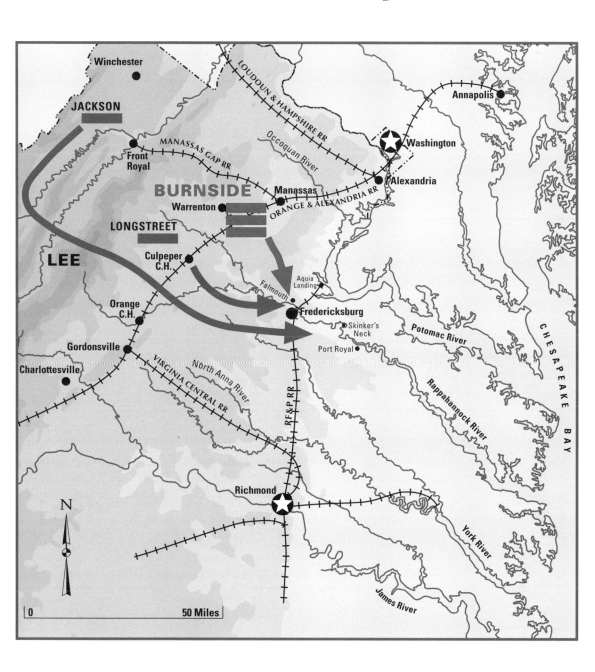

Burnside Crosses the Rappahannock, Dec. 11–13

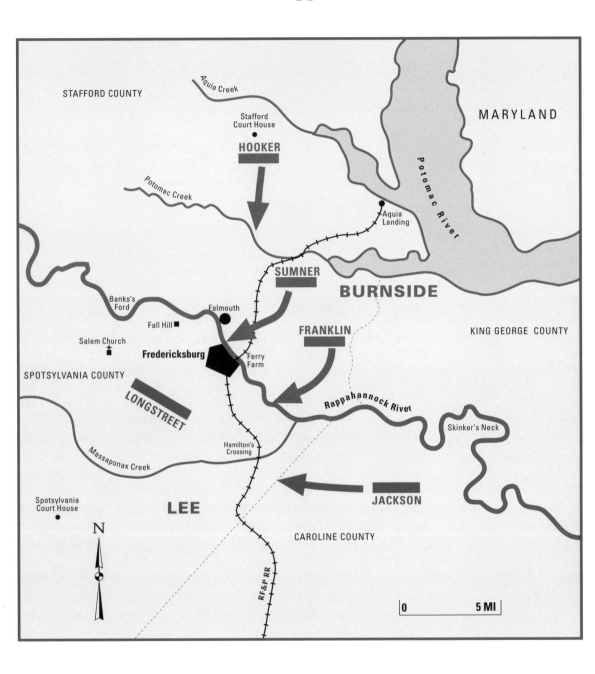

The Fighting at Prospect Hill

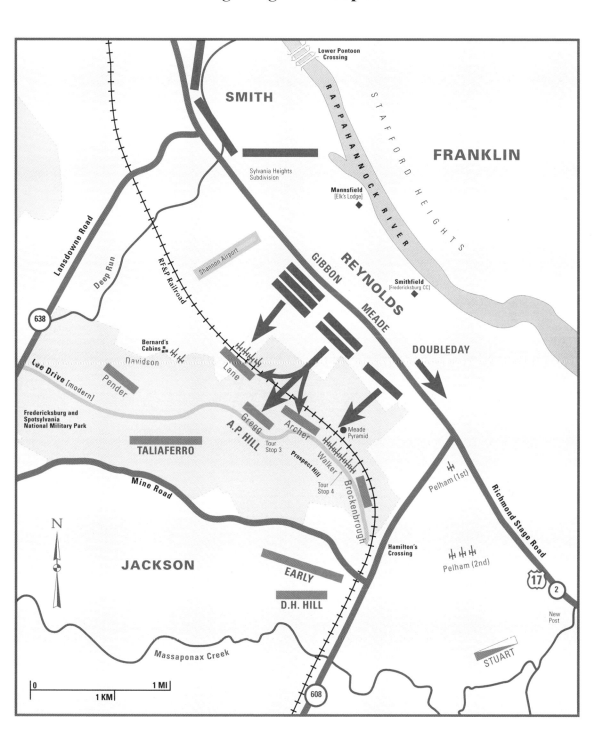

The Attacks on Marye's Heights

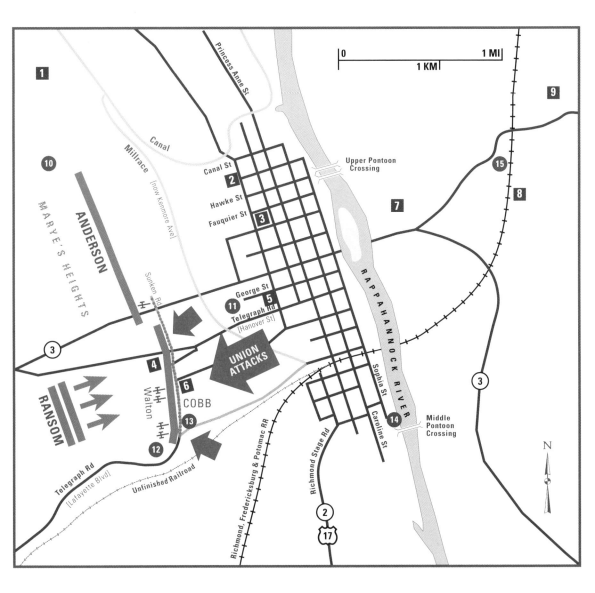

■ Historic Landmarks

1 Snowden
2 Mary Washington Tomb
3 Kenmore
4 Brompton
5 Federal Hill
6 Stephens House
7 Chatham
8 Falmouth Station
9 Phillips House

● Modern Landmarks

10 Mary Washington College
11 Maury School
12 National Cemetery
13 Fredericksburg Battlefield
   Visitor Center
14 City Dock
15 Earl's Hardware

McClellan takes leave of the army

George McClellan Bids the Army Farewell

Nov. 7, 1862, marked a beginning and an end for the Army of the Potomac. It marked the beginning of the Fredericksburg Campaign, and it marked the end of Gen. George B. McClellan's tenure as the army's commander. "Little Mac," as his men affectionately called him, had taken command of the Union's largest army more than a year earlier, in August 1861, following its defeat at Bull Run. Over the next eight months he had trained and reorganized the army, fashioning it into a formidable weapon. But McClellan soon demonstrated that he was more skilled at creating an army than in leading one. In a weeklong series of battles known collectively as the Seven Days, he had allowed his army to be driven back from the gates of Richmond by a much smaller Confederate force led by Gen. Robert E. Lee. When Lee then moved north into Maryland, McClellan headed him off Antietam Creek, near the town of Sharpsburg. In the single bloodiest day of fighting in American history, "Little Mac" compelled Lee's army to return to Virginia.

McClellan believed he had saved the Union. Upon closer inspection, however, it appeared that he had not so much saved the Union as squandered an opportunity to destroy the Southern army. At Antietam, Lee was heavily outnumbered and had his back to the Potomac River, making retreat difficult. Had McClellan been more aggressive, he could have smashed the Confederate army and brought a quick end to the war.

But, unfortunately for the Union, McClellan was a cautious man. Slow, sure movements were his way; bold risks and fast marches ran counter to his nature. At the heart of his caution was the unshakable belief that the Confederate army outnumbered him by a factor of at least two to one. No matter that reliable intelligence sources placed the number of Confederate soldiers at barely half his strength: McClellan continued to believe that he was heavily outnumbered. And, in his mind, an outnumbered general should not take chances.

So he continued to plod along, loved by his troops but doing little to end the war. That brought him into conflict with President Abraham Lincoln. Lincoln needed fighting generals who would bring the war to a speedy conclusion, and McClellan simply would not fight. Week after week the president prodded his idle general to advance and engage the enemy, but week after week "Little Mac" put him off, stubbornly refusing to risk his army in battle. The president tried to reason with the general. "Are you not over-cautious when you assume that you can not do what the enemy is constantly doing?" he asked. "Should you not claim to be at least his equal in prowess, and act upon the claim?" The president urged McClellan to stick close to the rebels and look for a chance to strike. "I would press closely to him,

George B. McClellan

fight him if a favorable opportunity should present, and, at least, try to beat him to Richmond on the inside track. I say 'try'; if we never try, we shall never succeed."

Still, McClellan refused to budge. In an effort to prod the general into action, Lincoln paid him a personal visit. The meeting only left the president more frustrated than before. As he started for Washington, he gazed back upon the sea of white tents stretched out behind him. Turning to an acquaintance, Lincoln asked, "Do you know what this is?"

"It is the Army of the Potomac," the man replied, a bit puzzled.

"So it is called," Lincoln replied, "but that is a mistake; it is only McClellan's bodyguard."

The president's patience clearly was wearing thin. When yet another month passed without a battle, he determined to rid himself of the popular general once and for all. On Nov. 7 Lincoln sent a War Department official, Gen. Catharinus P. Buckingham, to the army with orders relieving McClellan of command and appointing Gen. Ambrose E. Burnside in his place. McClellan took the news calmly. He viewed the situation as merely temporary. When Burnside failed (as McClellan was sure he would) and the Confederate army was threatening Washington, the Administration

would beg him to return. Until then, he would bide his time.

McClellan formally transferred command of the army to Burnside on Nov. 9, 1862. The news struck the army like a thunderclap. McClellan had been like a father to the soldiers, and news of his dismissal elicited strong emotion. Some officers resigned their commissions in protest; others called on McClellan to resist the order, march on Washington, and set up a military dictatorship. To his credit, the general refused to countenance such action and relinquished the command peacefully.

McClellan's final message to his army reflected his affection for his men. "In parting from you I cannot express the love and gratitude I bear to you. As an army you have grown up under my care.... The battles you have fought under my command will proudly live in our Nation's history. The glory you have achieved, our mutual perils and fatigues, the graves of our comrades fallen in battle and by disease, the broken forms of those whom wounds and sickness have disabled, — the strongest associations which can exist among men, — unite us still by an indissoluble tie. Farewell!"

Before departing for his home in New Jersey, the general held one last review of his beloved army. As he rode along the broad ranks of men, the soldiers cheered and threw their hats in the air. Others expressed their love by shedding tears. No one who experienced the scene was unmoved. "We have just come in from a funeral," wrote one officer, "the funeral of departed hopes. A more sorrowful time I have never seen in the army than just now."

No one felt McClellan's departure more sensibly than Ambrose Burnside, the genial Midwesterner on whose unwilling shoulders now rested the mantle of command.

Burnside and his senior generals

Ambrose Burnside Takes Command

Ambrose E. Burnside did not want the job. He had never wanted the job. Twice the President of the United States had asked him to take it, and twice he had refused. But this time was different. This time the president was not asking Burnside to take command of the Army of the Potomac; he was ordering him to do so. As a loyal officer Burnside could not refuse, though he made it clear that he accepted the command against his wishes. "Had I been asked to take it," he wrote the General-in-Chief Henry Halleck, "I should have declined; but, being ordered, I cheerfully obey."

Burnside was just 38 years old when he assumed command of the army. As a teenager, the Indiana native had become a tailor's apprentice, but the prospect of life in a workshop did not suit the boy's restless ambition, and at the age of 19 he enrolled as a cadet at the United States Military Academy. There he gained a reputation as a fun-loving, likeable chap. "Burnside was the idol of the class," remembered a fellow cadet, "our leader in everything but studies.... He was the soul of

'fun, frolic and friendship,' a model soldier in appearance, and so frank and manly that everybody trusted him." Burnside loved fun too much, perhaps. In his first year at the Academy he ranked 207th out of 211 cadets in conduct. The four who ranked below him on the list were sent home. Young Ambrose survived the cut, however, to graduate four years later, 18th of 38 in his class.

Upon graduation in 1847, Burnside became a second lieutenant in the artillery. The war with Mexico was just ending, and Burnside spent several months in Mexico City, wooing the senõritas and gambling at cards. Contemporaries noted that the young officer had a dangerous habit of raising the stakes when luck was running against him. By the time he left Mexico he found himself greatly in debt.

Bad luck was a theme of young Burnside's life. One tradition has it that he became engaged to a young lady from Ohio, but when the minister asked the flighty young woman if she would take Ambrose to be her husband, she replied, "No, sirree, Bob, I won't," and fled the room. (This same woman became engaged to another man a short time later. He apparently had heard about his fiancée's earlier engagement, for as the wedding began he drew a pistol from its holster, showed it to his bride, and announced that there would be "a wedding tonight or a funeral tomorrow." This time the woman fulfilled her pledge.)

Burnside had no better success in business. After leaving the army in 1853 he moved to Rhode Island and, borrowing some money, established the Bristol Rifle Works. Burnside produced a dependable carbine for the United

Ambrose E. Burnside

States Cavalry, but when the Secretary of War awarded the contract to another firm, the company went belly up. Deeply in debt, he turned to an old West Point friend for help. Like Burnside, George B. McClellan had left the United States Army to pursue a career in the private sector, but unlike Burnside he had succeeded. By 1858, McClellan was an executive with the Illinois Central Railroad. When Burnside wrote to him asking for assistance, he not only offered his friend a job with the company, but also allowed Burnside to stay at his home until he could get back on his feet. Thanks to McClellan's generosity, Burnside's future again looked bright.

The Civil War erupted just three years later. McClellan became a major general of Ohio volunteers, while Burnside was offered command of a regiment from Rhode Island. Both men enjoyed early success. In a series of small engagements, McClellan seized western Virginia (now West Virginia) for the Union, while Burnside — now a brigadier general — secured a foothold on the North Carolina coast. As a reward for his success, President Abraham Lincoln appointed McClellan commander of the North's largest army, the Army of the Potomac. Burnside, for his part, was bumped up to major general and eventually received command of the Ninth Corps, a unit in McClellan's army.

The war put a strain on the men's relationship. McClellan found Burnside slow (quite an indictment from a man who himself moved at a glacial pace) and blamed him for not promptly attacking at the Battle of Antietam. Stung by his friend's criticism, Burnside sulked.

McClellan too was coming under fire, however, and on Nov. 7, 1862, President Lincoln relieved him of command. In his place, he appointed Ambrose Burnside to lead the army. Lincoln had offered Burnside the position quietly twice before, but the modest general made it clear that he did not feel competent to hold such an important command. Others shared that view. "Those of us who were well acquainted with Burnside knew that he was a brave, loyal man," wrote Gen. Darius Couch, "but we did not think that had the military ability to command the Army of the Potomac." George Meade voiced a similar opinion about the likeable Midwesterner. "He had some very positive qualifications, such as determination and nerve," Meade noted to his wife, "but he wanted knowledge and judgment, and was deficient in that enlarged mental capacity which is essential in a commander."

That Burnside lacked the confidence and ability to command an army was undoubtedly true, but he had more personal reasons for not accepting the command. Doing so would have been a betrayal of his friend. So long as McClellan was in charge of the army, Burnside would not consent to replace him.

By November 1862, however, McClellan was no longer part of the equation. Gen. Catharinus P. Buckingham, the War Department official who brought Burnside the order to take command of the army, made it clear that the president planned to relieve McClellan regardless of whether Burnside accepted the position or not. The only question was who would replace McClellan. If Burnside refused the command, Buckingham had authority to offer it to Gen. Joseph Hooker. Burnside and Hooker disliked one another, and after much discussion Burnside finally agreed to take the job, if only to thwart Hooker's ambitions.

He accepted the position with the greatest reluctance. Meeting a fellow officer a couple of days later, Burnside remarked "that he had concluded to take command of the army, but did not regard the subject as one for congratulation." To anyone who would listen, he made it clear that he did not feel competent to lead the army. No one wishes to trust his life to a man who does not trust himself, and such statements only weakened Burnside's position. "He possessed an excessive self-distrust," wrote a Connecticut officer, "and it was creditable to his candor to confess it, and yet it is a question whether this distrust did not react unfavorably upon the officers and men of his command." George Washington had supposedly voiced similar self-doubts when he took command of the Continental Army in 1775. Would Burnside turn out to be another Washington? Or would he join Irvin McDowell, John Pope, and George McClellan on the growing list of Union generals who had ruined their reputations fighting on Virginia's "sacred soil"?

The Army of the Potomac Marches to Fredericksburg

Gen. Ambrose E. Burnside felt as if the weight of the world rested on his shoulders, and in a manner of speaking it did; for on Nov. 7, 1862, President Abraham Lincoln had appointed the affable Indiana native to command the Army of the Potomac. At 115,000 men, the Army of the Potomac was by far the Union's largest body of men. For more than a year it had been fighting Gen. Robert E. Lee's Confederates in Virginia and Maryland and rarely had it won. As the army's new commander, it was Burnside's job to change that. The question was "How?"

Burnside had accepted the command with the utmost reluctance, but once in the job he moved with uncharacteristic energy. His first step was to reorganize the army. At the time he took command, seven corps comprised the Army of the Potomac. Burnside felt that this was too many for one man to effectively wield in combat, and he promptly reorganized the army into three "grand divisions" of two corps apiece. (One corps, the Eleventh, remained unattached on duty in northern Virginia. On Dec. 9 the Twelfth Corps was added to the Eleventh to form the "Reserve Grand Division.")

To command the grand divisions Burnside se-

lected his three highest-ranking officers: William B. Franklin, Edwin Sumner and Joseph Hooker. Of the three, only Hooker had shown any aptitude for high command. Franklin was a protégé of McClellan's and like his mentor was cautious and slow. Sumner, by contrast, was a gallant old soldier of 65 winters, a former dragoon who would charge hell itself if ordered to do so. At Fredericksburg, he would do just that.

Opposing Burnside was a Confederate army of 78,000 men led by Gen. Robert E. Lee. The Southern army was dangerously divided. Half of it, under James Longstreet, occupied Culpeper, blocking a direct advance by Burnside on Richmond. The other half, led by "Stonewall" Jackson, lay across the Blue Ridge in the Shenandoah Valley, looking for an opportunity to sweep through the mountain passes onto Burnside's vulnerable lines of supply.

Conventional military wisdom dictated that Burnside attack and overwhelm Longstreet's corps before Jackson could come to its assistance. That was the plan of action McClellan would have taken — or so he later claimed. But Burnside had other ideas. Even if he defeated Longstreet, the Union commander reasoned, the Confederates

Fredericksburg

simply would retreat to a new line closer to Richmond. The closer Longstreet got to Richmond, the stronger he would become. Burnside, by contrast, would grow weaker as he advanced south because he would have to detail troops to protect his growing line of supply.

It was that line of supply that troubled Burnside the most. To feed, clothe and supply his massive army, Burnside relied on the Orange and Alexandria Railroad, which ran south from Alexandria to Gordonsville, thence south and east to Richmond. The railroad could hardly supply his army under the best of conditions. If Jackson, or Confederate cavalry, managed to cut the railroad even for a few days, Burnside's men and animals would face the prospect of starvation.

Then there was Washington, D.C. As commander of the Army of the Potomac, Burnside's top priority was to protect the capital. Advancing down the Orange and Alexandria Railroad via Gordonsville would pull Burnside west, away from the capital, making it vulnerable to a quick Confederate thrust.

In light of these difficulties, the new commander determined to shift his army to Fredericksburg and advance toward Richmond by way of the Richmond, Fredericksburg, and Potomac Railroad. The Fredericksburg route had much to recommend it. It would keep Burnside

closer to the Union-controlled rivers, thereby making it easier and safer to supply his army; it kept him between Lee's army and Washington D.C.; and it got him away from "Stonewall" Jackson's menacing presence.

In fact, there was only one drawback to the Fredericksburg route: the Rappahannock River. At Culpeper the Rappahannock is little more than a stream, fordable at any number of spots. By the time it reaches Fredericksburg, however, it broadens to a sizeable river, 400 feet in width, making it necessary to cross over a bridge. And that was the problem, for there were no bridges at Fredericksburg. The Confederates had destroyed them all earlier in the war.

The solution was to employ pontoons — portable bridges that floated on boats. The Army of the Potomac had a pontoon train, but unfortunately it remained at Berlin, Md., where the Army had used it a few weeks earlier to cross the Potomac River into Virginia. (A pontoon train consists of the boats, running gear, and other equipment necessary to transport and make a pontoon bridge.) No matter; Burnside would have officials in Washington simply send the pontoon train from Berlin to Aquia Creek, a branch of the Potomac River. From there, engineers could haul the pontoons overland the remaining distance to Fredericksburg.

Falmouth looking toward Fredericksburg

With that difficulty solved, Burnside submitted his plan to the president. Lincoln at first was cool to the proposal. After all, he had placed Burnside in charge in order to bring the Confederate army to battle. But now that Burnside was in command, he proposed to march *away* from the enemy and go to Fredericksburg. Lincoln sent two officers to Burnside's headquarters near Warrenton, Va., to discuss the matter. In the end, the general got his way. "The President has just assented to your plan," General-in-Chief Henry Halleck wired from Washington on Nov. 14. "He thinks that it will succeed if you move rapidly; otherwise not."

Rapid movement was not Burnside's strength. Like McClellan before him, he had what contemporary wags referred to as "the slows." But in this instance the general disappointed his critics by moving with unaccustomed alacrity. Gen. Edwin Sumner's Right Grand Division led the march. Breaking camp on Nov. 15, the old dragoon reached Falmouth in just two days' time. Across the Rappahannock River lay Fredericksburg, defended by a force of fewer than 1,000 men. While Northern guns threw shells into the town from a point near modern-day Falmouth Baptist Church, occupying the Southerners' attention, Sumner ordered the Irish Brigade to splash across the river at Falmouth and seize the town. The brigade was just entering the water when Burnside arrived. His marching columns then were scattered throughout Stafford County. Fearful that the river might rise and cut his army in two, Burnside ordered Sumner to recall his troops to the north bank. He would await the arrival of the pontoons.

A view of Falmouth from Fredericksburg

Hauling pontoons to Fredericksburg

The Case of the Missing Pontoons

At Fredericksburg, military success hinged on pontoons, those ungainly 5-foot-wide, 31-foot-long wooden boats used to construct temporary, floating bridges. When Gen. Ambrose E. Burnside took command of the Union Army of the Potomac in November 1862, he determined to shift his massive 115,000-man force from the vicinity of Warrenton, Va., to Fredericksburg. From there, he would advance toward Richmond, following the route of the Richmond, Fredericksburg, and Potomac Railroad (the modern CSX line) using the railroad and nearby navigable rivers to supply his army.

There was just one drawback to the plan: the Rappahannock River. As Burnside moved east, the Rappahannock broadened from a shallow stream to an unfordable river. By the time it reached Fredericksburg, it was 400 feet wide and impass-

able to troops. That's where the pontoons came in. If Burnside brought his own temporary bridges, he could cross the river quickly and seize Fredericksburg before Lee could march his army down from Culpeper to stop him.

Unfortunately, the pontoon boats and other bridging material (collectively known as the "pontoon train") had been left back at Berlin, Md., near Harpers Ferry, when the Union army crossed the Potomac River a few weeks earlier. Burnside knew this and had made arrangements through his boss, General-in-Chief Henry Halleck, to have the bridges sent from Berlin to Washington, thence via Aquia Creek to Fredericksburg. If all went according to schedule, the bridges would reach the tidewater town at the same time as Burnside's army, enabling it to cross the river without delay.

But in life things seldom go according to

schedule, and in government they never do. When the Army of the Potomac reached Fredericksburg on Nov. 17, 1862, the bridges were not there. In fact, as Burnside would soon learn, most of them were still back at Washington, more than 50 miles away. Until they arrived, his army could do nothing.

The delay was the result of bad communication, bad planning, and bad weather. To reach Fredericksburg, the engineers in charge the pontoon train had to float dozens of heavy boats down the C&O Canal towpath 50 miles to Washington. Once there, they had to assemble transportation for the train, then take it overland another 50 miles to Fredericksburg. A second train would go by water. The engineers had less than one week from the time they received the order to complete the job. It would be a Herculean task under the best of circumstances.

Pontoon boat on carriage

Poor communication hindered the operation from the start. It was Halleck's job to order the pontoon train to Fredericksburg. Lincoln had brought the general to Washington in July 1862 to provide unified leadership to the army's war effort. "Old Brains," however, proved to be more of a liability than an asset. Although a good organizer and military theorist, he had no aptitude for command and shunned responsibility of any kind. McClellan characterized him as "the most hopelessly stupid of all men in high position," while Secretary of the Navy Gideon Welles confided to his diary that Halleck "originates nothing...plans nothing, suggests nothing, is good for nothing." In the case of the pontoons, Halleck issued orders

for the pontoons to be sent to Aquia Creek, but he failed to impress upon the engineer in charge the importance of speed. Having given the necessary instructions, he ceased to concern himself with the matter.

After Halleck, primary responsibility for getting the pontoon bridges to Fredericksburg fell to Gen. Daniel Woodbury, commander of the army's Engineer Brigade. Woodbury received Halleck's order to send a pontoon train to Aquia Creek on Nov. 12. That same day one of Woodbury's subordinates, Maj. Ira Spaulding of the 50th New York Engineers, received an order from the Army of the Potomac directing him to ship the pontoons and bridging equipment to Washington. The order had been written a week earlier.

After consulting Quartermaster General Montgomery Meigs, Woodbury decided to send one pontoon train by land and the other by water. The water-borne train, led by Maj. J. A. Magruder, left Washington at 5 p.m. Nov. 16. Magruder lashed 48 pontoon boats together into a huge raft and towed them down the Potomac River behind a steamboat. Just below the capital the steamer ran aground on a sandbar. Even so, Magruder and his train reached Aquia Creek on Nov. 18, just one day after Burnside's army.

Spaulding's train did not fare so well. Before he set out Spaulding had to secure transportation for the train, including dozens of special wagons, 270 horses and harnesses, and teamsters. It all took time — lots of time. To make matters worse, when the horses arrived, Spaulding discovered that they had never been broken. Precious hours were

spent assembling the harness gear and getting the horses accustomed to wearing it. It was Nov. 19 before the land train was ready to go. Crossing the Potomac River via Long Bridge, Spaulding's pontoon train slowly wended its way south along the Telegraph Road (modern Route 1) amid a steady rain. Fifty miles away, on the Rappahannock River, the vanguard of Robert E. Lee's Army of Northern Virginia was marching into Fredericksburg.

For two days Spaulding's train toiled south on Telegraph Road amid unrelenting rains. The heavy boats and the muddy roads made progress tortuously slow. Three days out of Washington Spaulding reached the flooded Occoquan River. Another day was lost as he unloaded the heavy boats to construct a bridge across the swollen stream.

Spaulding was in a stew. By now, he realized that he was behind schedule and that the army was waiting for him. Rather than continue across country at a snail's pace, he lashed his 58 pontoon boats together into a large raft and had a ship from Washington pull it down the Potomac River to Aquia Creek, as Magruder had done several days before. The horses and wagons continued to Aquia Creek by land, but because they were now divested of their load they were able to move more rapidly.

Spaulding's flotilla reached the Fredericksburg area on Nov. 24; his horses and wagons arrived by land one day later. After two weeks of fighting treacherous sandbars, muddy roads and swollen creeks, the engineers finally delivered the bridges. Unfortunately they had arrived too late to do much good. The Confederate army had reached Fredericksburg five days earlier and now stood ready to contest the crossing. Burnside's campaign had foundered in the Virginia mud.

The Battle of Fredericksburg

Lee Rushes to Defend Fredericksburg

When Ambrose E. Burnside took command of the Army of the Potomac in November 1862, he did so with extreme reluctance knowing that he would have to take on Gen. Robert E. Lee. The 55-year-old Virginian had been in command of the Army of Northern Virginia for just six months, but in that time he had ruined the careers of two Union generals, George McClellan and John Pope. Burnside had no desire to be the third.

Lee could field 78,000 men, just two-thirds the number Burnside could muster, but with few exceptions his troops were hardened veterans of the Seven Days, Manassas and Antietam battles. A string of victories in 1862 had given the Confederates unbounded confidence in their leaders and in themselves.

Lee had divided his infantry into two corps, led by Gens. James Longstreet and "Stonewall" Jackson. When the Fredericksburg Campaign opened, Lee's army was dangerously divided. Longstreet's corps lay east of the Blue Ridge, near Culpeper, blocking the Union army's march to Richmond by way of the Orange and Alexandria Railroad. Jackson's half of the army was 60 miles away, on the other side of the mountains, near Winchester, Va., looking for an opportunity to slice behind the Union army and cut its supply lines with the North.

Burnside did not care for this arrangement, and upon taking command he rapidly moved his army from its camps near Warrenton to Falmouth. Once there, he intended to cross the Rappahannock River, seize Fredericksburg, and push on toward Richmond. But when he reached Falmouth, Burnside discovered that the pontoon bridges he needed to span the Rappahannock had not arrived. Rather than risk the destruction of his army by sending part of it across the river, he sat tight and waited for the bridges.

Burnside's march caught Lee flat-footed. Not until a Confederate force at Fredericksburg reported the enemy's arrival did he realize that the Union army had shifted eastward. Burnside had stolen a march on him. Confederate President Jefferson Davis urged Lee to defend the Rappahannock River line, but it seemed too late for that. Burnside's army had a two-day lead. By the time the Confederates reached Fredericksburg, the enemy would be across the river and pounding hard toward Richmond.

Lee accordingly set his sights on the North Anna River, the next defensible point between Fredericksburg and Richmond. On the North Anna's banks he would reunite the divided wings of his army and make a stand. To give himself time to reach the river, he sent two of Longstreet's divisions, commanded by Gens. Lafayette McLaws and Robert Ransom Jr., toward Fredericksburg to delay the Union army's advance. But when the two generals reached Fredericksburg, they found that enemy had not yet crossed the river. They reported this puzzling development to Lee, who promptly directed Longstreet's remaining three divisions to Fredericksburg. By Nov. 22, Longstreet's entire corps had reached the town. As a result of the pontoon train's delay, Burnside now would have to cross the river in the face of 40,000 Confederates rather than the 1,000 who had occupied the town before.

Robert E. Lee

Longstreet deployed his divisions on the hills behind Fredericksburg, just beyond the range of Union artillery on Stafford Heights. Dick Anderson's division held the northern end of the line, running from the Taylor house ("Fall Hill"), past John Stansbury's house "Snowden" (near modern Mary Washington Hospital), and across the ridge now occupied by Mary Washington College. On Anderson's right, Ransom's small division held Marye's Heights, where the National Cemetery and "Brompton" now stand. At that point, the Confederate line jumped back abruptly one-half mile to Telegraph Hill (now called Lee Hill), just beyond the modern intersection of Lafayette Boulevard and the Blue and Gray Parkway. McLaws's division held that part of the line, linking up on his right with John Bell Hood's and George Pickett's divisions. Hood's and Pickett's men extended the Confederate line south past Lansdowne Road to Hamilton's Crossing on the Richmond, Fredericksburg, and Potomac Railroad. In all, the Confederate line stretched for seven miles. It was among the strongest defensive positions held by Lee's army during the war.

Jackson's corps did not reach Fredericksburg for another 10 days. Using the discretion allotted to him by Lee, "Stonewall" lingered in the Shenandoah Valley looking for an opportunity to strike at Burnside's line of supply, just as he had done against another Union general, John Pope, three months earlier. Unlike Pope, however, Burnside did not give Jackson an opening. On Nov. 21, Jackson headed east to reinforce Longstreet's corps at Fredericksburg. It was a cold, grueling march, much of it over rocky ground. The shoeless Confederates suffered terribly. In an effort to alleviate their hardship, one of Jackson's division commanders, Daniel Harvey Hill, had his men wrap their feet in untanned hides taken from slaughtered cattle. Unfortunately, that didn't work. The soldiers slipped on the slushy roads as if on ice, and when the leather footwear dried it stiffened to such a degree that it became positively painful to wear. The soldiers finally kicked off the ersatz moccasins in disgust, preferring to wrap their bruised and bloody feet in rags or straw. The soldiers gained one thing from the experience, however: a new nickname for their commander. From then on, Hill was known derisively as "Old Rawhides."

Jackson's corps reached Fredericksburg on Dec. 3, having covered 175 miles in just 12 days. The general deployed his troops south of town, covering the Rappahannock River between Hamilton's Crossing and Port Royal. With the arrival of Jackson's corps, Burnside lost whatever slim chance he may have had for success. Lee now had his entire army at hand and held a nearly impregnable position on the hills in back of the river. Burnside would need a good plan to overcome such disadvantages. Unfortunately, the Union commander no longer had a good plan; indeed, as of early December, he had no plan at all.

Burnside Ponders His Options

Ambrose Burnside was in a quandary. The newly christened commander of the Army of the Potomac had brought his troops to Fredericksburg with the intention of crossing the Rappahannock River and pressing on to Richmond. Upon reaching the tidewater town; however, he discovered that the pontoon bridges that he needed to span the river had not arrived. Burnside could have sent his troops wading across the river at Falmouth or at one of several upriver fords, but getting his supply wagons and artillery trains across was another matter. To Burnside's way of thinking, there was no choice but to wait for the pontoons.

They arrived a week later, but by then it was too late. James Longstreet's corps of Lee's army — 40,000 men — had reached Fredericksburg and stood ready to contest any attempt Union forces might make to cross the river. The Union commander pondered his options. Upriver from Fredericksburg stood Banks' Ford, but Longstreet's troops covered the ford, and the river's steep banks there favored defense. (Banks' Ford is located near the spot where River Road today grazes the Rappahannock River.) Above Banks' Ford, the Rapidan River split off from Rappahannock, giving Burnside two broad rivers to cross rather than one. Had he succeeded in forcing his way across the river there, he would enter the Wilderness, a dense second-growth forest that would hem in his army and make it difficult to maneuver. All things considered, it was

perhaps best to leave the upriver crossings alone.

Then there was Fredericksburg itself. Although Longstreet's pickets guarded the tidewater town, Union artillery on Stafford Heights (near Chatham and Ferry Farm) could brush them aside easily, or so it was thought. It was after Burnside's army crossed the river that the trouble would start. Longstreet's divisions occupied the heights behind the town, and it would be no easy matter to drive them off, particularly since "Old Pete" had fortified the hills with cannons and entrenchments.

There was one other option: a crossing down river from Fredericksburg. After flowing past the colonial town, the Rappahannock meandered back and forth until it reached Port Royal, where it broadened into an estuary. A crossing below Port Royal was infeasible due to the width of the river, but a crossing above the town just might work. Not that a crossing there would be easy. The ground north of the Rappahannock between Fredericksburg and Port Royal was choppy and contained many steep ravines. Creeks would have to be bridged and roads improved before the army could move. It would be hard to keep such work a secret from the prying eyes of local inhabitants, who would be all too willing to pass the information on to Lee. Even if Burnside did force his way across the river, he still might find Confederates blocking his path on the hills beyond.

The downriver route offered two distinct advantages, however. First, there was no sizeable body of Confederates at that point to contest the crossing. Scouts reported a few Confederate horsemen there, but one or two well-placed shots by a Union battery would scatter them quickly. Second, if Burnside could throw his army across the river quickly, he might succeed in getting between the Confederate army and Richmond. Lee would have no choice but to attack him. Otherwise he would risk losing the city and with it his source of supplies.

Burnside made his plans accordingly. The spot he selected for crossing the Rappahannock was Skinker's Neck, a flat, fertile area hemmed in by a large bend in the river. (Local golfers will recognize this as the site of Four Winds Golf Course.) No sooner had Union engineers begun improving the approaches to the river there, however, than Confederate infantry appeared — thousands of them. Lee obviously had guessed Burnside's intentions and shifted part of Longstreet's corps to Skinker's Neck to meet the crossing. Or so it must have seemed to the bemused Union commander. What actually had occurred was that "Stonewall" Jackson's corps — the missing half of Lee's army — finally had arrived and was going into position south of Fredericksburg.

With the arrival of Jackson's men, Skinker's Neck no longer seemed so inviting. Still Burnside had to do something. The Northern people expected him to bring Lee to battle before winter,

Darius N. Couch

and he would not let them down. The weather had been unusually mild so far, but that was about to change. On Dec. 5, the skies dropped four inches of snow on the ground. It would melt away quickly, but its significance was clear: winter was just around the corner.

With time running out, Burnside revised his plans. Rather than cross at Skinker's Neck, as he had intended, he would cross at Fredericksburg itself. The Confederate army held a 20-mile line — from the fords above Fredericksburg to Port Royal. To cover such a large area, it had to be stretched thin. If Burnside could throw his army across the river at Fredericksburg before Lee could concentrate troops there to meet an attack, he just might cut the Confederate army in two and achieve the victory he sought.

Burnside called his grand division commanders to a council of war on Dec. 9 and explained his plan. William Franklin and Joseph Hooker opposed the scheme, while loyal old Edwin Sumner expressed a willingness to undertake anything that Burnside proposed. Sumner's subordinates were not so compliant. For three weeks they had watched the Confederates strengthen their position on the hills behind the town. They knew that Burnside was leading them into a slaughter pen, and they did not hesitate to say so. "...There were not two opinions among the subordinate officers as to the rashness of the undertaking," recalled

Gen. Darius Couch.

Burnside got wind of his subordinates' objections and confronted them at Sumner's headquarters the next evening. "I have heard your criticisms, gentlemen, and your complaints," one officer remembered him saying. "You know how reluctantly I assumed the responsibility of command. I was conscious of what I lacked; but still I have been placed here where I am and will do my best. I rely on God for wisdom and strength. Your duty is not to throw cold water, but to aid me loyally with your advice and hearty service...." Couch replied that "no matter what might be my opinion as to the feasibility of the maneuver that he would find no one more ready than myself to aid him in the enterprise." Others voiced similar sentiments. If Burnside did not have the enthusiastic support of his officers, at least he could rely upon them to obey his orders.

As word of Burnside's proposed advance trickled down through the ranks, a feeling of doom pervaded the army. "Your father has determined to cross immediately," Sumner's son-in-law wrote his wife, "...and his staff all feel that they are to march into the jaws of death itself. Time can never efface the impression they all gave me of their almost sure and certain destruction." Sgt. John Holahan of the 45th Pennsylvania Volunteers expressed similar foreboding. "'On to Richmond' has prevailed over reason and we must go!" he confided to his diary. "Well, go we will, but not without apprehension. Those terrible heights before us are enough to terrify, but we will do our best...."

That evening, as the hour for the crossing the Rappahannock drew nigh, portions of the army left their camps and crept closer to the river. Col. Samuel K. Zook did not expect to return. As he gazed across watery divide toward the dreaded heights, now teaming with Confederate gun pits, he could not shake a sense of personal doom. Grabbing a pen, he scribbled off a final note to his son. "I expect to be sacrificed tomorrow," he wrote. "...Goodbye old Boy & if tomorrow night finds me dead remember me kindly as a soldier who meant to do his whole duty."

Confederates on the railroad bridge

Before the Storm

The Army of the Potomac reached Fredericksburg in mid-November 1862, but it did not attempt to cross the Rappahannock River until Dec. 11. The Union troops made good use of their time building corduroy roads across the muddy Virginia terrain, reconstructing the wharves at Aquia Landing, and repairing the Richmond, Fredericksburg, and Potomac Railroad between Aquia Landing and Falmouth. Building a new bridge across Potomac Creek was the greatest challenge to putting the railroad in operation, but Union engineers set their minds to the task and by Nov. 28 the trains began to run.

The Confederates also were busy during those weeks, constructing earthworks along the river and on the hills behind the town. Among the works were nine gun pits built for the Washington Artillery. These small, crescent-shaped works oc-

cupied the brow of Marye's Heights, one-half mile behind the town. Cannon inside them could scour the plain that extended from Fredericksburg to the heights. Gen. James Longstreet commanded that part of the line. When he recommended that the artillery commander in that sector squeeze another gun onto the heights, the officer replied: "General, we cover that ground now so well that we will comb it as with a fine-tooth comb. A chicken could not live on that field when we open on it." A bit of an exaggeration, perhaps, but not much, as events would show.

Both sides sent spies across the river in an effort to discover the position and intentions of the opposing army. At the same time Union signalmen intercepted messages transmitted by their Confederate counterparts, who were wig-wagging messages up and down the line by means of large flags. The Confederate signalmen knew that they were being watched and transmitted their messages in code. What they didn't know was that the Union signalmen had broken the code. Even so, the intelligence coup produced little useful information.

The weather was unusually balmy in the weeks leading to the battle. But on Dec. 5 a cold front swept in from the north, drenching the countryside with a pouring rain. Temperatures dropped and by late afternoon the rain switched to sleet, then to snow. By the following morning four inches of white powder covered the ground. The weather turned bitterly cold. Soldiers'

Trading with small sailboats

hands and beards froze; water turned to ice; a few soldiers literally froze to death while standing picket near the river.

The Confederates suffered the most, having the fewest supplies. Some were without shoes, most lacked adequate clothing, and none had yet been issued tents. "They manage to eke out some kind of shelter, either with oil cloths [rubber tarps], or a blanket over poles, or brush-wood covered with leaves," wrote Gen. William Nelson Pendleton. "And by dint of good out of doors fires, and many lodging together they are enabled, I hope, to sleep in tolerable warmth. At best, though," he admitted, "it is a rough business."

Union soldiers had adequate supplies of clothing and blankets and therefore suffered less. But the freezing temperatures still had their effect. A Union soldier huddled over his campfire recorded his discomfort in the pages of his diary: "Feet are aching, noses biting, ears and fingers tingling." The frigid temperatures, wrote another, were "enough to cool down the most ardent patriotism." Soldiers farsighted enough to build winter huts found their tiny homes packed with guests

seeking to keep warm. "We're too thick to be welcome," noted one intruder, "but we don't mind slight rebuffs — we take them good-naturedly and stay until crowded." The cold front soon passed, however, and temperatures again increased. By the time the Union army would cross the river, daytime temperatures were back into the 50s.

That was good news for Union and Confederate soldiers assigned to picket duty along the Rappahannock. By tacit agreement, opposing pickets agreed not to shoot at one another unless one side or the other attempted to cross. For several weeks they walked their beats in full view of one another, occasionally stopping to converse or to exchange barbs across the watery divide. Some soldiers rigged up toy sailboats. When the wind was right, Confederates would send small amounts of tobacco plying across the river. Union pickets gratefully pocketed the fragrant cargo, and when the wind shifted they sent back coffee in return. Officers eventually put a halt to the illicit trade.

Relations between opposing pickets became so chummy that in rare instances soldiers from one army actually crossed the river to talk and trade newspapers with their counterparts on the other side. One Confederate got more than he bargained for. When he reached the Stafford shore, he was assaulted by a man who had been his enemy long before the war. To avenge the insult, Johnny Reb's friends opened fire on the Yankees, killing several. Such behavior was an anomaly, however. For the most part pickets scrupulously honored the informal truce.

During periods of inactivity, boredom became the soldiers' worst enemy. Some Confederates relieved the tedium by paying visits to residents in town, where they received a cordial reception and a warm meal. Others engaged in sports and games. Union pickets, gazing across the shimmering river, watched as Confederates played baseball, competed in foot races, and held boxing tournaments.

On the heights in back of town, the Washington Artillery erected a stage and sold tickets to an open-air theatrical production. Using logs for seats and tent flies for curtains, the hardened veterans performed "The Lady of Lyons," a play popular at the time. A lieutenant played the lead role with Sgt. John Wood acting the part of the heroine, Pauline. "The play went off admirably well," remarked one amateur critic, "but where the sergeant got his petticoats from he won't tell!"

This peaceful interlude terminated abruptly in December. Despite the approach of winter, the Northern people clamored for an advance on Richmond. Bowing to public pressure, Union commander Ambrose E. Burnside ordered a crossing of the Rappahannock on Dec. 11. The long-awaited offensive was about to begin.

Banjo player in camp

Building bridges under fire

The Battle of the Bridges

Gen. Ambrose Burnside had made his decision. The Union Army of the Potomac would cross the Rappahannock River at dawn, Dec. 11, 1862, and storm the Confederate position on the hills behind Fredericksburg. The plan's success depended on speed and surprise. Gen. Robert E. Lee had deployed his Confederate army over a 20-mile area, from the fords above Fredericksburg, on the left, to Port Royal, Va., on the right. Lee's position was strong, but if Burnside attacked quickly, before Lee had time to bring his troops together, he might be able to punch a hole in the Confederate line and gain victory. It all depended on a speedy passage of the river.

Burnside planned to span the river at three points. He ordered his engineers to lay two bridges at the foot of Hawke Street, in the northern end of town; one at the city dock, just below the railroad bridge; and two more at a point one mile below Fredericksburg, near the modern Bowman Center. Construction of the pontoon bridges

was to begin at 3 a.m. As the hour approached, large wagons carrying the pontoon boats crept quietly toward the river bluffs. Engineers, working in silence, slid the boats off the wagons and man-handled them down the steep slopes toward the river's edge. The first boats entered the water and were anchored to the shore. Other boats followed, the engineers connecting them by means of timbers and planks. The bridges slowly began to take shape.

A few hundred feet away, on the opposite shore, Confederate soldiers were listening. In order to give him early warning of a crossing, Lee had posted sentries, known as pickets, all along the riverbank. Those in Fredericksburg belonged to Gen. William Barksdale's Mississippi brigade. Although darkness and a heavy fog prevented Barksdale's men from seeing the Union engineers, their ears clearly told them what was taking place. Soldiers went from door to door, urging the few remaining civilians in town to flee, while a horseman dashed to Lee's headquarters to deliver news of the crossing. A short time later a Southern artillery battery fired two shots in rapid succession: a pre-arranged signal alerting the army that the enemy was in motion.

The Union engineers heard the shots and understood their meaning. Their pace quickened. By now, the first rays of sunlight were beginning to appear in the east, yet the bridges were still more than 100 feet from the Confederate shore. Capt. Wesley Brainerd had charge of one of the two upper bridges. "I was standing at the extreme outer end of the bridge encouraging my men," he recalled, "when, happening to cast my eyes to the shore beyond just as the fog lifted a little, I saw, what for the moment almost chilled my blood. A long line of arms moving rapidly up and down was all I saw, for a moment later they were again obscured by the fog. But I knew too well that line of arms was ramming cartridges and that the crisis was near."

A moment later, the Confederates opened fire. "The bulletts [sic] of the enemy rained upon my bridge," Brainerd remembered. "They went whizzing and spitting by and around me, pattering on the bridge, splashing into the water and thugging through the boats." As soon as the firing started, the engineers sprinted toward the Stafford shore and threw themselves face down in the mud to escape the leaden hail. Many, Brainerd noted, did not make it. "Some fell into the boats, dead. Some fell into the stream and some onto the bridge, dead. Some, wounded, crawled along on their hands and knees and in a few moments all of us were off the bridge, all except the dead.... It was simple murder, that was all."

In an effort to provide a cover fire for the engineers, many of the 147 cannon arrayed across Stafford Heights opened fire on the town. When the Confederate fire slackened, Union engineers made a second, then a third, attempt to complete the bridges. Each time the Mississippi riflemen drove them back to the Union shoreline. Casualties mounted. Among them was Brainerd, who received a bullet in the arm. Gen. Barksdale

Confederate sharpshooters

reportedly sent word back to Lee saying "if he wants a bridge of dead Yankees [I] can furnish him with one."

Gen. Daniel Woodbury commanded the brigade to which the engineers belonged. Endowed with more courage than sense, Woodbury repeatedly ordered his troops back out onto the river. After several failed attempts, they refused to go. "I was greatly mortified...to find that the pontoniers under my command would not continue at work until actually shot down," he reported with astonishment. "The officers and some of the men showed a willingness to do so, but the majority seemed to think their task a hopeless one. Perhaps I was unreasonable."

Meanwhile Ambrose Burnside grew more and more frustrated. He had not anticipated such staunch resistance, and he had no clear idea of how to overcome it. In desperation, he ordered his artillery to bombard the town. For eight hours, northern cannon poured shot and shell into the unfortunate town, shattering walls and setting houses on fire. When Union gunners on the bluffs reported difficulty in depressing the muzzles of their guns low enough to strike the buildings along the waterfront, artillery chief Henry Hunt ordered 36 pieces down to the water's edge, where they blasted the town at point-blank range. "Tons of iron were hurled against the place," wrote one unfortunate Mississippian. "...The deafening roar of cannon and bursting shells, falling walls and chimneys, brick and timbers flying through the air, houses set on fire, the smoke adding to the already heavy fog, the bursting of flames through the housetops, made a scene which has no parallel in history. It was appalling and indescribable, a condition which would paralyze the stoutest heart, and one from which not a man in Barksdale's Brigade had the slightest hope of escaping."

Damage to the town was immense. "Fredericksburg is all knocked to pieces," wrote one soldier. "Every house almost is full of holes where the shells have been sent. Possibly it may be repaired again but I think [it] doubtful." A Georgian who toured the shattered town after the battle was shocked at the thoroughness of the destruction. "There is scarcely a house in the town that has not some mark of the siege," he wrote home. "Chimneys knocked off, roofs torn up, and walls scarred with holes of various sizes, some as large as a man's head and others as large as a flour barrel.... The large tall houses suffered more than the low buildings. A large Baptist Church [Fredericksburg Baptist Church] has fifteen large holes through the walls, four through the steeple and the roof torn up in many places. I think there are twenty five or thirty houses burned."

Some Mississippians were struck by shells or crushed by falling masonry, but others stubbornly hung on and continued to fight. By afternoon, the Union army was no closer to crossing the river than it had been at dawn. Time was running out. If Burnside was going to get across the river, he had to employ a different strategy. But what? Gen. Hunt offered a suggestion: Send pontoon boats filled with soldiers across the Rappahannock and push the Confederates back from the water's edge. The plan was fraught with peril, but Burnside had no choice. At 3 p.m., he ordered the assault.

Bombardment of Fredericksburg

The Battle of Fredericksburg

Crossing the river under fire

Fighting in the Streets of Fredericksburg

The Battle of Fredericksburg was unique in many ways: It was the largest battle in North America up to that point, it featured the first cross-river landing under fire in American history, and it was the first instance of urban warfare in America. The Union army shelled Fredericksburg on Dec. 11, 1862, after Mississippi riflemen led by Gen. William Barksdale thwarted its efforts to throw pontoon bridges across the Rappahannock River. The bombardment failed to dislodge the Confederate sharpshooters, however, and about 2:30 p.m. Union commander Ambrose E. Burnside ordered troops to cross the river in pontoon boats and seize the town.

The task was fraught with peril. Hundreds of Confederates held the town, firing from the protection of cellars, barricades, and shallow earthworks built along the river's edge. To reach the town, Union troops would have to cross the river in open boats, form a hasty line of battle on the Confederate side, and charge into town, all the while exposed to a murderous fire. It was a task to daunt the most fearless heart.

Because of the danger involved, Gen. Burnside asked for volunteers. Col. Norman J. Hall stepped forward. Just 25 years old, Hall had seen more action than many men twice his age. As a young lieutenant fresh out of West Point, he had taken part in the defense of Fort Sumter, S.C. After serving briefly on the staff of the Army of the

Potomac's chief engineer, Hall was appointed colonel of the 7th Michigan Infantry Regiment. By December 1862, he led a brigade in the Second Corps. Brave and eager for glory, he offered the services of his troops in making the desperate attempt. Hall's old regiment, the 7th Michigan, would spearhead the assault.

The crossing began shortly after 3 p.m. Under the cover of a heavy Union bombardment, two companies of the 7th Michigan readied boats along the Stafford shore. When the firing stopped, the soldiers dashed from their places of concealment along the riverbank, shoved the 31-foot-long pontoon boats into the water, and began rowing and poling with all their might. Some 70 men went across in the first wave, led by Lt. Col. Henry Baxter. As the small craft raced across the muddy river, bullets struck the water around them and splintered the sides of the boats. Baxter and several others were hit, but casualties as a whole were remarkably light. Just one man was killed in the initial crossing.

The boats touched shore at the foot of Hawke Street. (Today the National Park Service owns a small parcel of land there, marked by a monument and historical sign.) The Michigan soldiers jumped out of the boats and formed a hasty skirmish line in the shelter of the river bluff then charged up into town. Smashing down doors, they entered the houses that lined the river and drove out the Confederate sharpshooters. "The orders were to give no quarter," remembered one Union participant, "but for humanity's sake, we did not obey them...." Within minutes, the 7th Michigan had scooped up 31 prisoners and secured a toehold along Sophia Street.

Additional troops were needed if the 7th Michigan was to hold the town. While the regi-

ment engaged the enemy in house-to-house combat, the pontoon boats returned to the Stafford side of the river and brought over two companies from the 19th Massachusetts. The Bay State troops deployed to the right of the 7th Michigan, expanding the bridgehead one block north, to Pitt Street.

The pontoon boats continued to ferry back and forth across the river with additional reinforcements, enabling Hall to solidify his grip on the town. Union soldiers on Stafford Heights cheered as each new boatload of troops reached the contested shore. "It was a display of heroism, which moves men as nothing else can," wrote a Massachusetts soldier. "The problem was solved. This flash of bravery had done what scores of batteries and tons of metal had failed to accomplish."

William Barksdale

Much hard fighting remained before the Union army could claim success, however. Barksdale's men fought doggedly, contesting each house, each yard, each woodpile. "Nearly every house and cellar had some one in it, firing from the windows," a Union officer asserted, "but we soon cleaned them out." Sometimes a body of Confederates would conceal themselves in a cellar or attic, wait for the Union soldiers to pass, then shoot at them from the rear. Bullets seemed to come from all directions from an invisible foe. "The most dangerous and trying part of the action," thought one Union soldier, "was that the enemy could fire a volley at such close range without being seen."

One Northern company lost 10 of 30 men in five minutes. The fighting waxed hottest along Caroline Street, which the Confederates had turned into a stronghold. They not only occupied the buildings along the street, but also had erected barricades made of earth and stone between buildings. For nearly two hours they held their ground against the growing number of Union soldiers in their front.

The task of breaking the impasse fell to the 20th Massachusetts. Known as the "Harvard Regiment," the unit included sons of some of Boston's finest families. Pushing the boats across the river by means of poles, it formed in rear of the 7th Michigan and 19th Massachusetts. At orders from Hall, the regiment, 307 strong, advanced down Hawke Street in a lengthy column that had the appearance and function of a human battering ram. The massed body of men, hemmed in by houses on the left and right, made a perfect target for Barksdale's soldiers. When the head of the regiment reached Caroline Street, the Confederates unleashed a torrent of fire that staggered the regiment and nearly annihilated the leading platoon. Nevertheless the regiment pressed ahead. One group of men charged across the intersection and engaged the Confederates beyond. Other companies wheeled to the left and right at the intersection, only to be decimated by a murderous fire. In less than 30 minutes, the 20th Massachusetts lost 97 men.

By now the pontoon bridges had been completed, and Hall's remaining regiments charged across, extending the Union line as far south as William Street. At the same time, a second Union brigade crossed the Rappahannock at the lower end of town, at the modern city dock, and threatened to turn the Confederates' flank. With darkness stealing over the contested town, Barksdale decided that he had done enough. He ordered his men to fall back to the main Confederate line, located on Marye's Heights.

The 21st Mississippi covered the retreat. The fighting flared briefly when one of its officers discovered that an old college chum commanded the Union forces in his front. Unwilling to give ground to his erstwhile friend, the Southern officer halted his troops and counterattacked. Ignoring orders from his superior officer to fall back, the renegade officer continued to attack and had to be placed under arrest. His replacement continued the retreat, and by evening Fredericksburg was in Union hands.

Capturing the town had come at a heavy price. Barksdale's stubborn stand had cost the North hundreds of men and had given Lee time to concentrate his forces on the heights outside of town. As Ambrose Burnside soon would learn, in taking Fredericksburg he had stepped into a trap.

Dead Confederate pickets

Drummer boys at Fredericksburg

The Drummer Boy of the Rappahannock

Robert Henry Hendershot was a rambunctious boy. No, he was more than rambunctious; he was downright rebellious. Hendershot had grown up in Michigan at a time when that state was still something of a frontier. His father died when he was just a few years old, leaving his mother to rear him alone. He was the sort of child every parent dreads. "Robert had always been of a high-strung temperament," his biographer H.E. Gerry explained, "with a force of willpower and temper hard to govern. He did not like attending school, absenting himself without leave or ceremony, and in preference hunted watermelon patches, fished, skated, blacked boots, sold papers, in fact anything suited to his fancy which was directly in opposition to the wishes of his mother and the family at home."

The Civil War gave Robert an outlet for his adventuresome spirit. In the fall of 1861, a company from Hendershot's town left the state and headed to the front. Although he was under age, the boy tagged along. Time and again, the officers sent him home, but each time he came back. As Gerry noted, "The officers were destined to find the little warrior a persistent fellow, and decidedly hard to get rid of."

Hendershot eventually joined Company B, 9th Michigan Infantry. In a skirmish at Murfreesboro, Tenn., he was captured and sent to Camp Chase, Ohio, to await exchange. The impetuous youth had no intention of wasting time in an exchange camp, however, and he slipped away and re-enlisted in the 8th Michigan Infantry on Aug. 19, 1862, under an assumed name, Robert Henry Henderson.

The 8th Michigan belonged to the Army of the Potomac, and Hendershot soon found himself on his way to Virginia. He joined his new regiment on Nov. 28, just in time for the Battle of Fredericksburg. In an effort to seize the town, Union commander Ambrose E. Burnside ordered the 7th Michigan Infantry Regiment to cross the river in pontoon boats under fire and drive Confederate riflemen from the Fredericksburg waterfront. Although Hendershot was in the 8th Michigan rather than the 7th, he tried to climb into one of the first boats as it pushed off from shore. Instead, he slipped and fell into the icy water. Rather than give up, he grabbed on to the boat and was dragged across.

When the boats touched shore, the 7th Michigan dashed into town and engaged the Confederates in house-to-house combat. Robert had a different agenda. Following in the wake of his adopted regiment, he "went into a house and set it on fire, stole a clock, two blankets, and some other small articles." Somehow he managed to get the purloined items back to his camp in Stafford County. Grabbing a discarded rifle, he then returned to Fredericksburg for additional booty. "He went into a different house," wrote Gerry, "and assisted in destroying mirrors, pianos, and other valuable property." He had just applied a match to another residence and was heading out the back door when he encountered a rebel with a shotgun. Hendershot had the drop on him and demanded the man's surrender. At the prompting of some other soldiers, he then personally escorted his prisoner to the rear, presenting him to Gen. Burnside in person at the Lacy House (Chatham). The Union commander praised the boy for his gallantry. "Well, boy," he was quoted as saying, "if you keep on in this way...you will soon be in my place." Hendershot was then just 12 years old. Burnside advised the youngster to return to camp, but Hendershot replied that he "preferred to go and capture another Johnny Reb." Inspired by his spunk, the general and his staff raised "three cheers for Robert Henry Hendershot... the Drummer Boy of the Rappahannock." The nickname stuck.

Hendershot remained at the front and was

Robert Hendershot

wounded slightly two days later in the Union attacks on Marye's Heights. As a result of the wound, and possibly his age, he was discharged on Dec. 27. By then, Hendershot's fame had spread across the country. When he reached Washington, Northern citizens hailed him as a hero. He dined with President Lincoln at the White House and appeared as a guest at both houses of Congress. Later, when he visited New York City, the New York *Tribune*'s editor, Horace Greeley, presented the lad with a fancy new drum. Capitalizing on the boy's popularity, showman Phineas T. Barnham engaged Hendershot to play his drum at Barnham's museum. Over time, a poem and a play were written about Hendershot, extolling his courage.

Hendershot enjoyed his celebrity status and milked it for all it was worth. In the decades following the war he performed on his "Greeley

Drum" at meeting halls throughout the nation. At Wa-Keeney, Kan., more than 200 people turned out to hear the now-middle-aged drummer play. (Apparently Wa-Keeney was starved for entertainment.) Miss Ruth Welch, a local dignitary, brought the house to its feet with a stirring recital of the poem "The Drummer Boy of the Rappahannock," after which the curtain opened and Hendershot appeared, beating his drum to the tune, "Marching Through Georgia." His son played the fife at his side. The crowd went wild, wrote a *Western Kansas World* reporter, calling for encore after encore until Hendershot "had far more than exhausted the pieces which had been so industriously published as constituting his part of the program."

The only ones not enamored with Hendershot were the soldiers of the 7th Michigan Infantry, the regiment that had stormed Fredericksburg. No one in that regiment remembered seeing Hendershot on Dec. 11, 1862. In their estimation the real hero of the fight was their own drummer boy, John S. Spillane.

In 1891, the Grand Army of the Republic (an association of Union veterans) held its national meeting in Detroit and invited Hendershot to take part in its parade. The 7th Michigan was outraged by the invitation and publicly challenged Hendershot to produce even one witness who had

Robert H. Hendershot and his son, J.C. Hendershot

seen him at Fredericksburg. "Failing this, we feel ourselves justified in declaring in a public manner our belief that this claim is a fraud," its members declared. Hendershot answered his critics the following night at a reunion of the 7th Michigan. Taking the stage, he produced letters from President Lincoln, Gen. Grant, and Horace Greeley attesting to his bravery. But none of those men had been at Fredericksburg, his critics countered; they had. Did any of the 200 veterans in the room know Hendershot? When no one rose to Hendershot's defense, pandemonium broke out. "Throw him out of the window!" cried one man. The crowd seemed at the point of doing just that, when the 7th's own drummer boy, John S. Spillane (then a captain on the Detroit police force), entered the room. "There," shouted a veteran, "there is the drummer boy of the Rappahannock!" The veterans hustled Spillane to the platform and unceremoniously booted Hendershot down the stairs. After the meeting, the citizens of Detroit presented Spillane with a medal proclaiming him, not Hendershot, to be the real "Drummer Boy of the Rappahannock."

Was Hendershot a hero or a fraud? As is so often the case with history, we shall never know. The witnesses, like the tap of Robert Henry Hendershot's drum, have fallen silent.

Fredericksburg civilians return home

Caught in the Crossfire: Civilians at Fredericksburg

Fredericksburg was an old and dignified town, even in 1862. Nestled close to the Rappahannock River, its 5,000 inhabitants enjoyed an easy, comfortable existence. Although places like Richmond and Alexandria had taken away much of Fredericksburg's trade, the establishment of several new mills and the construction of a narrow-gauge railroad leading to Orange, Virginia, gave promise to more prosperous times ahead.

The national crisis that engulfed the country in 1860 divided Fredericksburg, as it did many communities in the country. Most residents wished to remain in the Union as long as the constitutional liberties of the South — that is, slavery — were protected. States in the Deep South were not quite so willing to compromise, however, and in the wake of President Abraham Lincoln's election in November 1860, many of them voted themselves out of the Union and established the Southern Confederacy. Virginia remained in the

Union until April 1861, when South Carolina forces fired on Fort Sumter. President Lincoln declared the South in a state of rebellion and called on the loyal states to supply 75,000 troops to defend the Union. Forced to choose between her brethren in the North and the South, Virginia sided with the South.

The war had little direct impact on Fredericksburg until April 1862, when 30,000 Union troops pushed south from Washington and occupied the town. Abraham Lincoln visited Fredericksburg in May to confer with Gen. Irvin McDowell about future military operations. Under McDowell's lenient tenure, local citizens suffered few indignities or hardships. War's iron fist had not yet landed on the tidewater town.

That changed in December 1862 with the arrival of Gen. Ambrose E. Burnside's Army of the Potomac. Fredericksburg residents watched in dismay as division after division of Union soldiers appeared on Stafford Heights. "Watched with trembling hearts the long line of Yankees pouring over the Chatham hills to take the same station they occupied last summer," wrote one resident. "They come in countless number and our hearts sank within us."

Three days later, Lee's army began to arrive, bringing with it the promise of imminent conflict. The Confederate leader urged Fredericksburg residents to evacuate their homes and sent army wagons and ambulances to speed their departure. Many citizens boarded trains and headed toward Richmond. Five hundred ended up at Milford Station, 15 miles south of town. Compassionate Caroline County residents sent carriages to bring refugees to their homes. Some houses took in as many as 30 people.

As days passed with no sign of a Union crossing, many Fredericksburg residents returned to their homes. The sound of two cannon shots fired at 5 a.m., Dec. 11, startled them from their sleep. The Army of the Potomac was crossing the river! Confederate soldiers ran from house to house pounding on doors, urging residents to flee. Grabbing blankets to protect them from the winter chill, women, children and old men hurriedly left their homes and trudged out of town. Some stayed at the homes of friends who lived in the country; others gathered at outlying sanctuaries like Salem Church. Many simply camped in the woods, throwing up a blanket or a piece of carpeting for shelter. "It made me feel so sad this

evening to see an old man and Lady supporting a sick son," a Confederate officer confided to his diary, "and just behind them were an old white man and an old black woman leading him, he being blind...."

Some civilians did not move quickly enough and were caught in the Union bombardment later that day. As houses caught fire, terrified families dashed through the streets searching frantically for a safe haven. They found none. Jane Beale was asleep at her home at 307 Lewis Street when the artillery fire jarred her awake. Hastily gathering her family, she took refuge in the cellar of the house. They could hear shells shrieking and crashing through the roof and upper rooms above. "I shall never forget to the day of my death, the agony and terror of the next four hours," she wrote. Each minute "was burnt in on my memory as with hot iron. I could not pray, but only cry for mercy." A minister who was staying with the family began to read from the 27th Psalm: "Tho an host should encamp against me, my heart shall not fear...." No sooner had he spoken these words than a 12-pound cannonball crashed through the wall, shattering glass and splintering a timber. Miraculously no one in the room was seriously injured.

Toward evening, Beale's brother banged on the cellar door. The Yankees had crossed the river, he informed them; they had to get out. Ignoring the danger, the family left the dark cellar and piled

Shell explodes inside Fredericksburg cellar

The Battle of Fredericksburg

into a military ambulance. Excited horses whisked them away at a full gallop down Hanover Street to the Telegraph Road (now Lafayette Boulevard). Just past Marye's Heights, near modern "Dead Man's Curve," the vehicle passed a crowd of woman and children who had taken refuge near a mill on Hazel Run. The women were weeping and the children crying, Beale noted.

Refugees huddled around a fire

"I saw one [woman] walking along with a baby in her arms and another little one not three years old clinging to her dress and crying 'I want to go home.' My heart ached for them, and if I could I would have stopped the Ambulance and taken them in, but I did not know then that I might not have to spend the night out in the open air myself...."

In their hurry to exit the town, some families got split up. A soldier in the 21st Mississippi Infantry regiment was pulling out of town when he encountered a little girl in the fire-swept streets. Scooping the infant up in his arms, the rough soldier raced back to the main Confederate line on Marye's Heights.

By Dec. 12, Fredericksburg was firmly under control. Union soldiers who occupied the town broke into buildings looking for food and plunder. In several houses, food remained half-eaten on the table, showing the haste with which the residents had left. For four days Union troops occupied the town, using the buildings as barracks or as makeshift hospitals.

Civilian casualties were surprisingly light. Fewer than half a dozen residents appear to have been killed in the battle. The destruction of property, on the other hand, was immense. The buildings in town had been shelled, ransacked, then turned into hospitals. Fires had destroyed some of the structures; artillery shells and human malice had severely damaged the rest. "Almost every house has six or eight shells through it;" wrote resident Betty Herndon Maury, "the doors are wide open, the locks and windows broken, and the shutters torn down. Two blocks of buildings were burned to the ground." Like most buildings, Maury's house had been used as a hospital. "Every vessel in the house...[was] filled with blood and water...the table in the parlour was used as an amputating table, and...a Yankee (Byron Pearce of N.Y.) was buried at the kitchen door."

Maj. W. Roy Mason lived at the "Sentry Box" on lower Caroline Street. After the battle he discovered three dead Union soldiers in his home, including one whose form had left a bloody imprint on the floor of the parlor that would last for many years. The corpses of five or six others had been buried in the yard outside. That was not uncommon: the entire town had become a graveyard.

There was at least one happy ending, however. The day after the Union retreat, the soldiers of the 21st Mississippi marched back into Fredericksburg, carrying on their shoulders the little girl they had rescued five days before. As they entered the town, a young woman dashed up to the officer who was holding the child, screamed, and fainted into his arms. They had found the toddler's mother.

The Sacking of Fredericksburg

The Sacking of Fredericksburg

By the time the fighting ended on Dec. 11, Fredericksburg was desolate. Fighting in the streets combined with a bombardment by more than 180 cannons had left the venerable old town shattered and ruins. Those citizens who had not fled Fredericksburg had seen their homes riddled with bullets, shot and shell.

Worse was yet to come. On Dec. 12, the Union army crossed the Rappahannock River in force, occupying Fredericksburg and the plain south of town. Hour after hour the troops crossed, the heavy tread of their shoes causing the pontoon bridges beneath their feet to sway gently back and forth. The endless columns of men with their shiny rifles and colorful flags presented an image of power and invincibility. "Whomsoever would say to me at that time that anything else but certain victory awaited this army, I would have looked upon him with scorn and contempt," wrote Captain John Donovan of the Irish Brigade. "I was not aware that hell personified was so close at hand and ready for our destruction."

Just how close became evident later that day when Confederate gunners on the hills behind Fredericksburg began to drop shells near the bridges. The projectiles narrowly missed their targets, plunging into the river and showering troops with a spray that one man considered "cooling, but not refreshing." Although shell fragments injured dozens of soldiers, the crossing continued.

The band of 122nd Pennsylvania Volunteers took a position at the foot of a bridge. It had just started to play the tune "Bully For You" when the Southerners opened fire. For a moment there was panic, as band members scattered for cover. One musician took a ribbing from his friends for seeking shelter behind his bass drum. "It was about as much protection as a sheet of paper," laughed one soldier.

The bombardment was an unpleasant reminder what lay ahead. The Confederates held a strong position, and Union soldiers knew that hundreds — even thousands — of men might die trying to capture it. Undertakers knew it too, and as the Union columns crossed the river one enterprising mortician stood at the foot of the bridges handing out business cards. His aggressive marketing angered some of the soldiers, and they finally drove him off. Thoughts of death were less easy to dispel, however, and as soldiers crossed the river many threw away their playing cards. Gambling was considered a sin, and no soldier wanted to face his Maker with a deck of cards in his pocket. By the end of the day, thousands of cards littered the bridges.

Once across the river, Union soldiers engaged in a more lucrative pastime: the search for tobacco. Tobacco was a scarce commodity in the North, selling for about two dollars a pound. When Union soldiers learned that city authorities had dumped a large shipment of the fragrant leaf into the Rappahannock River, willing hands plunged into the frigid waters next to the city dock and brought it up. Soon every man had as much as he could carry.

The Union crossing lasted throughout the morning and into the afternoon. Soldiers with time on their hands broke into shelled-out houses looking for food, tobacco or some small token of the town. What began as minor pilfering quickly degenerated into wholesale pillage. For a few hours discipline and order vanished as soldiers dashed from building to building, stealing whatever they could find. "The ladies [of Fredericksburg] said before the battle they would sooner see the city destroyed & their homes made desolate forever than to see it surrendered to us," crowed one Union soldier. "We have accommodated them in every particular for there is not a building left untouched in the whole city."

Soldiers took whatever caught their fancy, unmindful of how they would get it home. A Connecticut soldier saw his comrades leave houses carrying absurd and often worthless plunder: a stuffed alligator, a pair of brass andirons, an apothecary's pestle, musical instruments, and even mouse traps — "everything that was ever made to eat, drink, wear or use." Financial institutions were a favorite target of the thieves. A group of particularly determined soldiers managed to crack

the safe at the Bank of Virginia, where they found silverware, half dollar coins, and a large quantity of currency. "...Everything valuable was carried away," wrote an approving lieutenant.

Theft gave way to vandalism and wanton destruction. Soldiers bayoneted paintings, smashed mirrors and china, hurled glasses through windows, pulled down draperies, and tore up carpeting. Books from private libraries were hurled into the muddy streets; barrels brimming with flour were turned over and poured out onto the floor. "The soldiers seemed to delight in destroying everything," wrote one witness. The widespread pillaging reminded a New Hampshire soldier of incidents in previous wars. "I had read in history where the Grecian army entered Troy and where Napoleon had entered Moscow with the French army, and how those cities were given up to pillage; but never had the real meaning of war come to me until now."

The soldiers tore Fredericksburg residences apart with a savage glee. Some grabbed chairs, lounges and beds and smashed them into kindling for their fires. Others, caught up in the frenzy of destruction, manhandled rosewood pianos into the streets then set them on fire or battered them to pieces. "Vandalism reigned supreme," wrote one disgusted artilleryman. "Men who at home were modest and unassuming now seemed to be possessed with an insatiate desire to destroy everything in sight."

Some soldiers donned women's clothing and paraded down the street with parasols and bonnets, adding a bizarre twist to the chaotic events of that day. "It was a rich scene," thought a Minnesota man. "There was a dirty soldier dressed in the choicest silks, escorted by other soldiers dressed in long tail coats, and plug hats.... One of the boys picked up a violin, and a soldier was soon found who could play it, so they took positions for a cotillion.... But I cannot do justice to the scene." A chaplain put the best face on the matter, claiming, "This was simply the spirit of eternal youth exemplified, the thing that kept men's hearts from 'failing them.'"

Decent men voiced outrage at the proceeding. "...The conduct of our men and officers...is atrocious," wrote Quartermaster John Godfrey. "Their object seems to be to destroy what they can't steal & to steal all they can." "...The sacking our soldiers gave the city was shameful," agreed a surgeon. "The town was fairly turned inside out. Not a nook or crevice...but was ransacked." Soldier Tully McCrea expressed outright revulsion at what was going on. "I never felt so much disgusted with the war as I did that day."

The sacking of Fredericksburg was the most disgraceful episode in the Army of the Potomac's history. Second Corps historian Francis Walker tried to justify the soldiers' actions, insisting that in plundering the town the army had done "nothing contrary to the laws of war." Because the town had refused the army's demand to surrender and had to be taken by assault, he argued, "the conquerors had the right to sack and pillage. At the same time," he added with a twinge of conscience, "it would be pleasanter to remember Fredericksburg had nothing of the sort taken place."

The sacking of Fredericksburg

The Battle of Fredericksburg

Final Preparations

Ambrose Burnside still had no very clear idea of what to do. The general commanded the 115,000-man Union Army of the Potomac. For three weeks the army lay poised in Stafford County awaiting its commander's orders to cross the Rappahannock River and strike the enemy. Gen. Robert E. Lee's Confederates meanwhile were busy constructing earthworks on the heights behind the town. Burnside finally made his move on Dec. 11, throwing three sets of bridges across the river at Fredericksburg. After a massive bombardment followed by hours of house-to-house fighting, the town finally had fallen to the Union. Gen. Edwin B. Sumner's Right Grand Division, 30,000 strong, tramped across the upper bridges on Dec. 12 and occupied Fredericksburg. At the same time, Gen. William B. Franklin's Left Grand Division filed across another set of bridges one and one-half miles below town and deployed in the fields along the Richmond Stage Road (Route 2/17) near modern Shannon Airport. After glaring at one another across the Rappahannock River for nearly a month, the two sides were ready to come to blows.

Gen. Robert E. Lee held the upper hand. Although Burnside significantly outnumbered Lee's 78,000-man army, the Confederate leader occupied a formidable defensive position on the heights behind the town. Southern engineers had improved the position with gun pits and trenches. If Lee only could bring together enough men to hold this strong position, victory would follow.

Initially, however, the Confederate chieftain was not certain that Burnside intended to make his main effort at Fredericksburg. "Stonewall" Jackson's corps, comprising half of the Southern army, covered the area between Fredericksburg and Port Royal, 15 miles down river. Lee brought up two of Jackson's four divisions on Dec. 11, the day the Union army bridged the river, but he left the troops of Gens. Jubal Anderson Early and Daniel Harvey Hill back at Port Royal, just in case Burnside's crossing at Fredericksburg proved to be a decoy to cover a crossing farther downstream.

On Dec. 12 Sumner's grand division poured down the heights near Chatham and occupied Fredericksburg in force. At the same time, Franklin's grand division pounded across the wooden pontoon bridges south of town and took position along the Richmond Stage Road. Any doubts Lee may have had about Burnside's intentions vanished at the sight of this immense host. Couriers from headquarters galloped south with orders for Early and Hill to bring their divisions to Fredericksburg with all haste.

The Confederate commander spent the rest of the morning riding his lines, making final preparations for the coming clash. By afternoon he was back at his command post on Telegraph Hill conferring with subordinates and awaiting his opponent's next move. (After the war Telegraph Hill was renamed Lee Hill in the general's honor. It is located on the northern end of the park tour road, Lee Drive, at Tour Stop No. 2.)

Lee's opponent, Gen. Burnside, had no idea what that move would be. Having successfully fought his way across the Rappahannock, the Union commander hoped that Lee might give up the heights without further bloodshed. When Lee confounded those hopes by staying put, Burnside seemed to be at a loss. It was obvious to Gen. Darius Couch that his superior "had no fixed plan of battle. After getting in the face of the enemy, his intentions seemed to be continually changing."

On the afternoon of Dec. 12, as his troops wantonly ransacked the town, Burnside searched in vain for a promising point of attack. He had no good options. Lee's army occupied the heights west and south of town. Its left flank was anchored on the Rappahannock River at the Taylor house, "Fall Hill" (near modern Bragg Hill Apartments), and his right flank tied into Massaponax Creek south of town (near the community of New Post). Burnside could not turn his opponent's flanks without returning to Stafford County and recrossing the Rappahannock elsewhere. It was too late for that; besides, Lee would simply shift his army to meet the new crossing.

Unable to get at Lee's flanks, Burnside had no choice but to make a frontal assault. The Union commander scanned the Confederate line with his telescope, looking for weaknesses. He found none. On Lee's left, north of town, the Confederate line ran along a precipitous ridge, the same one now occupied by Mary Washington Hospital. In front of the ridge was the Fredericksburg canal. In order to attack Lee's left, Union troops would have to bridge the canal not once but twice, form in the open under a severe artillery fire, then storm the ridge. The chances of success were slim.

The Confederates continued to hold the ridge south of this point, their line running straight through the middle of modern Mary Washington College's campus. The ground at the foot of the hills — near modern Kenmore Park — was so marshy that Burnside considered it militarily impassable.

South of that point was Marye's Heights. Although it too was formidable, as Union troops

would learn soon to their grief, an attack there had one great advantage. Because the heights were immediately behind the town, Union troops would have less ground to cross in order to reach the Confederate line than at any other point on the field. Less ground meant fewer casualties.

South of Marye's Heights the Confederate line curved gently away from the Union lines, forming what modern military analysts call a "pocket." Pockets are dangerous places to attack because they subject attacking troops not only to a frontal fire but to fire on both flanks — in short, a crossfire. Even Ambrose Burnside knew better than to attack there.

That left just one other spot: the far right end of the Confederate line, a place known locally as Prospect Hill. (Today Prospect Hill lies at the end of Lee Drive, at Tour Stop No. 4.) There, just

short of Massaponax Creek, the Confederate line again flattened out and the heights were less lofty. A strong attack there might break Lee's line, placing the Union army between Lee and Richmond.

Burnside reviewed his options and issued his orders. Franklin would attack Confederate forces led by "Stonewall" Jackson at Prospect Hill and drive them off the ridge, while Sumner, to his right, attacked Gen. James Longstreet's corps on Marye's Heights thereby preventing Longstreet from reinforcing Jackson. In pugilist terms, Burnside planned to throw a left hook followed by a right jab. Gen. Joseph Hooker, commanding Burnside's Center Grand Division, would remain on Stafford Heights in reserve, ready to pursue the defeated Confederates once Franklin and Sumner had broken their lines. It was a blueprint for victory — or a recipe for disaster.

Franklin's Crossing

William B. Franklin and the Trials of Command

One can hardly blame William Buel Franklin. He was trained to be an engineer not a general. Yet at the Battle of Fredericksburg Franklin found himself in charge of no less than 40,000 troops — fully one-third of the Union army. It was an odd position for a man who just six months earlier had never commanded troops in combat.

Like most Civil War generals, Franklin was a product of West Point. The 39-year-old Pennsylvanian had graduated first in the class of 1843, the same class in which Ulysses S. Grant had graduated 21st. As a result of his superior academic standing, Franklin had the privilege of selecting his branch of service, and he chose the engineers. No one expected him to do otherwise. After all, engineers were paid more than other soldiers, and they often received plum assignments in the East rather than being sent to isolated frontier posts like their unfortunate counterparts in the infantry or cavalry.

Specifically, Franklin was a topographical engineer. This elite group of men did mapping for

the army and oversaw government construction projects. Franklin was a precise, methodical man, and he excelled in such work. Prior to the Civil War he surveyed the Great Lakes region and produced one of the first maps of the Oregon Trail. Later he was assigned to duty in Washington, where he oversaw construction of the U.S. Capitol dome and a wing of the U.S. Treasury Building.

Franklin's reputation stood high in 1861, and when the Civil War began he was appointed colonel of the 12th U.S. Infantry. As the army grew, so did Franklin's responsibilities. By October 1861, he was a brigadier general in charge of a 10,000-man division, and eight months later he was placed in command of Army of the Potomac's newly-christened Sixth Corps.

Franklin owed his advancement, in part, to his friendship with the army's commander, Gen. George B. McClellan. "Little Mac" and Franklin had much in common. Both were West Point graduates who had graduated at or near the top of their class and both had become army engineers.

Both were highly intelligent but cautious men. McClellan considered his friend "one of the best officers I had. He was perhaps a little slow to move," he suggested, "but very powerful when the machine was in motion. He was a man of excellent judgment and a remarkably high order of intellectual ability. He was in all respects an admirable corps commander."

Ambrose Burnside also held a high opinion of Franklin. Burnside replaced McClellan as the Army of the Potomac's commander in November 1862. In one of his first acts as commander, he reorganized the army, grouping its eight corps into three "grand divisions" of two corps apiece. Franklin, as one of the army's ranking officers, received command of the Left Grand Division, consisting of the First and Sixth corps. Although he had been with the army for 18 months and had taken part in several campaigns, Franklin still had not seen much combat. Chance always seemed to place him on the fringe of the action. It would be unfair to say that Franklin was a stranger to battle by the time the Union army reached Fredericksburg, but at best the two were passing acquaintances.

Franklin's Left Grand Division crossed the Rappahannock River below town on Dec. 11, just upriver from the modern Sylvania Heights subdivision. Compared to Gen. Edwin Sumner, who had to fight tooth and nail to secure a toehold in Fredericksburg, Franklin crossed the river with ease. Confederate forces on Franklin's front had no cover and therefore were unable to seriously contest his passage.

Those who tried were scattered quickly by the fire of Union artillery on Stafford Heights. At Burnside's orders, Franklin sent just one brigade across the river on Dec. 11; the rest of his force crossed the following day. By noon, Dec. 12, Franklin had his grand division hunkered down by

William B. Franklin

the river protecting his pontoon bridges.

With his troops safely across the river, Franklin met with his two corps commanders, Gens. John F. Reynolds and William F. "Baldy" Smith, to analyze the military situation. Upon examining the Confederate position, they concluded that the Union army should attack the right end of the Confederate line, near Hamilton's Crossing, and attempt to turn Lee's flank. They urged this movement on Burnside, who met with them at 5 o'clock that evening. The commanding general seemed agreeable to the plan, but he wished to give it some more thought. He promised to send Franklin and his officers written instructions within three hours.

Three hours passed, then six, then nine. At 3 a.m., Reynolds announced that he was going to bed. "I know I have hard work ahead of me and I must get some sleep. Send for me if I am wanted." Finally around 7:30 a.m., Dec. 13, Burnside's orders arrived. Written two hours earlier, the disjointed dispatch directed Franklin to send out "one division at least" to "seize" the heights near Hamilton's Crossing, "taking care to keep it well supplied and its line of retreat open." Sumner would attack Marye's Heights at the same time. Seizing both heights, Burnside hoped, would "compel the enemy to evacuate the whole ridge between these points."

Like all engineers, Franklin was an exact man, and Burnside's rambling orders left him confused. He had expected to make a major assault; instead his chief appeared to want something much smaller, an attack by "one division at least." Franklin perused the paper again. Burnside's orders directed him to "seize" the heights. In the military parlance of that day, you seized an undefended or lightly defended position; you carried a strongly held position. Moreover, Burnside seemed to lay great emphasis on Franklin protecting his line of retreat over the pontoon bridges. Putting all this together, Franklin concluded that Burnside no longer wanted him to attack the heights in force, as he had indicated earlier, but simply to make an "armed reconnaissance." His literal translation of Burnside's orders would have far-reaching consequences.

One has to wonder why Franklin did not seek clarification of his orders before beginning his attack. A portable telegraph connected Franklin's headquarters with those of Burnside, reducing the time it took to communicate to a matter of minutes. But Franklin made no effort to clarify his ill-worded orders. Maybe he was miffed at Burnside for taking so long to get his instructions to him or perhaps he felt there wasn't time. Some critics have suggested that Franklin wanted Burnside to fail so that he could inherit the army command. Whatever his motives, Franklin had been ordered to move "at once," and he would brook no delay. For good or for ill, he would follow his orders to the letter.

Telegraph operator at work

Artillery in action

The Gallant Pelham

The Battle of Fredericksburg produced many heroes, but none more celebrated than blond-haired, blue-eyed Maj. John Pelham. At age 24, Pelham commanded the Army of Northern Virginia's horse artillery, the light guns that traveled with the Confederate cavalry. Young ladies liked Pelham because of his handsome features and winning personality; his fellow soldiers admired his bravery and modesty. Pelham was attending the United States Military Academy when the Civil War began. Leaving West Point, he traveled south and enlisted in a Confederate artillery battery. There he caught the eye of Gen. J.E.B. Stuart, the Army of Northern Virginia's chief of cavalry. Stuart took an instant liking to the young man (who was scarcely five years younger than himself) and appointed him to command the cavalry's lighter, faster-moving horse artillery. At the Seven Days, at Antietam, and at many smaller actions in between, Pelham harassed the Union army with his cannons.

The young man's fame reached its zenith at Fredericksburg. Pelham was with Stuart on the far right of Lee's line, near Massaponax Creek, when the Union army began to deploy on the plain ahead. The troops belonged to Gen. George G. Meade's Pennsylvania Reserves. Earlier in the day, Meade had received orders from his commander,

Gen. John F. Reynolds, to attack Confederate forces occupying a wooded ridge south of town. Meade led his division to a point opposite Smithfield plantation (now the Fredericksburg Country Club), then wheeled right to cross the Richmond Stage Road (now known as the Tidewater Trail). Thick hedgerows and deep drainage ditches bordered the road, delaying Meade's progress. Pioneers with shovels and axes quickly removed these impediments, and by 10 a.m. Meade was ready to begin his assault. His line stretched across the fields now occupied by the General Motors Powertrain factory.

John Pelham watched the Union deployment with growing excitement. Meade's troops faced west, toward the wooded heights, placing Pelham directly on their left flank.

Seeing an opportunity to do the enemy some damage, Pelham received permission from Stuart to advance one gun to the intersection of the Richmond Stage Road and the road that led to Hamilton's Crossing (modern Benchmark Road). Once there, he opened fire with solid shot. The iron projectiles bounded down the length of the line, creating havoc in the Union ranks. One shot struck a Northern cannon; another exploded an ammunition chest. Meade's foot soldiers threw themselves face down in the muddy field for cover.

One Pennsylvanian remembered "pressing down hard...and flattening out that I might not interfere with any of the flying iron."

For a minute or two Pelham had things his own way, but Northern artillerymen quickly recovered from their surprise and fought back. Eighteen cannon on the plain showered the Confederate major with shot and shell. Across the Rappahannock River, Union cannon on Stafford Heights added their weight to the bombardment. Pelham had stirred up a hornet's nest.

John Pelham

Stuart sent a second gun forward to assist his protégé, but it no sooner joined the action than a solid shot struck it, knocking it out of action. Pelham would have to go it alone. That was just to the dashing young Alabamian's liking. Pelham concealed his gun from enemy sight by placing it behind intervening hedgerows. When Union cannon began zeroing in on his position, he would shift position and continue firing. Despite his attempts at evasion, the Union fire began to have its effect. Men and horses began to fall at a frightening rate. Three times Stuart sent couriers to Pelham ordering him to retreat. Each time the messages were ignored. "Tell the General I can hold my ground!" he gamely told one courier.

Finally Pelham exhausted his ammunition and retired to the safety of his own lines. He had fought successfully against long odds, delaying Meade's assault by more than half an hour. Witnessing Pelham's exploit from Prospect Hill, Lee remarked: "It is glorious to see such courage in one so young!" He praised his brave subordinate in his report of the battle and recommended his promotion to lieutenant colonel.

Pelham's greatest praise, however, came from George Meade, who later insisted that he came under attack from an entire four-gun Confederate battery rather than Pelham's solitary piece. As a result of Pelham's actions, Reynolds detailed Gen. Abner Doubleday's division to guard his left flank, thus immobilizing 6,000 men who might have been used to advantage elsewhere.

Today a state historic marker and a small granite monument at the intersection of the Tidewater Trail and Benchmark Road mark the site of the Pelham's gallant exploit. In addition, the Central Virginia Battlefields Trust Inc., has purchased a small plot of ground nearby in order to preserve it for future generations of Americans. Pelham himself did not survive the war. He died on March 17, 1863, at Kelly's Ford, in Culpeper County, impetuously leading a cavalry charge. It was a fitting, if tragic, end for the young man known throughout the army as the gallant Pelham.

The Pelham Monument

Union artillery south of Fredericksburg, May 1863

Union Artillery Pounds Prospect Hill

Four miles south of Fredericksburg, at the end of the battlefield tour road, stands a cannon-studded knoll known as Prospect Hill. Today the hill is a quiet, peaceful place, but in 1862 it was the scene of a fierce duel between artillerymen of the Blue and the Gray. John Fulton Reynolds, commanding the Union army's First Corps, had orders to take the hill, a task he delegated to Gen. George G. Meade's division of Pennsylvania Reserves. As Meade aligned his men for the attack, Maj. John Pelham of the Confederate army brought forward a lone cannon and began shelling Meade's left flank. Union artillery drove away the annoying Confederate, allowing Meade to proceed with the assault.

Pelham's was not the only Confederate cannon on the field, however. Meade knew that the wooded ridge ahead harbored dozens of additional guns. Before ordering his troops to attack, he resolved to knock out any Confederate guns that might be lurking there. He directed artillery chief Col. Charles Wainwright to shell the heights.

The bombardment began at 11 a.m. Wainwright opened fire with four batteries totaling 18 guns. Union artillery across the Rappahannock River on Stafford Heights added their weight to the attack. For an hour, wrote one witness, "the air was resonant with the savage music of shells and solid shot." The Union gunners fired at a slow, steady rate. Three months earlier, at the Battle of Antietam, Wainwright's boss, Gen. Henry J. Hunt, had watched in disapproval as gun crews rapidly fired off their ammunition so as to be able to leave the battlefield. He was not going to let that happen again. At Fredericksburg he ordered gun crews to fire no more than one round every three minutes. Firing at a more rapid pace, he sternly lectured, would be viewed as evidence of cowardice.

At the height of the bombardment, the Federals had as many as 60 guns in action. The shelling was impressive in terms of the noise and smoke it generated, but it failed to draw out and destroy Confederate artillery on the ridge. Stonewall Jackson had approximately 50 guns on his portion of the line, but he wisely had ordered his men to withhold their fire until the Union army sent forward its infantry. Because Jackson's artillery did not reply to his bombardment, Wainwright could not tell where the Confederate guns were, much less whether he had damaged any of them.

Jackson's gunners finally tipped their hand about noon. As Meade aligned his division for the attack, he pushed forward the 9th Pennsylvania Reserve Regiment as skirmishers. Capt. David G. McIntosh, commanding a Confederate artillery battery on Prospect Hill, watched breathlessly as the Union line approached. "What an awful suspense these last moments are," he later recalled. "The gun is charged, lanyard in hand, the gunner at the trail, ammunition heaped in piles nearby, waiting for the order to fire. Minutes seem like hours. One holds his breath and then breathes hard. But at last the moment comes." Eight hundred yards in front of the Confederate guns stood a lone tree. Southern artillerymen had measured its distance precisely and cut the time fuses on their exploding shells accordingly. When the Union line reached the tree, 14 guns let loose with a roar. "From then on," McIntosh wrote, "it is load and fire, load and fire, as fast as sponge and rammer and lanyard can do their work, and as fast as muscle and skill and consuming zeal can direct and control...."

By firing on the Union line, the Confederates exposed the position of their guns to Union view. Wainwright once again ordered his cannon forward to shell the heights. There was now no reason for the Confederates to hold back, and for an hour both sides went at it hammer and tongs. The Union army had superior artillery and ammunition, and the Confederates took a beating. The 14 guns at Prospect Hill were especially hard hit. In the ranks that day was a young South Carolina soldier named Ben. As he stood by his gun, iron fragments struck all around him. "The trees around our guns were literally torn to pieces and the ground plowed up," he informed his parents. "I have been several times covered with dirt, and had it knocked in my eyes and mouth."

Willie Pegram

Three men in Ben's battery died in the maelstrom; 16 others were wounded. Ben himself survived by only the narrowest of margins. "A piece of shell went through my coat sleeve; it stung a little," he recalled. "A Minié ball went through the ramrod, and it or a splinter struck me on the head. I was by the gun looking at the Yankees when a great piece of shell, big as my two fists, came along and knocked a spoke out of the wheel, and it or a piece of the spoke, or something else, hit me square in the breast.... I saw a piece of shell go a 'kiting' by my leg, missing it an inch or two. This is only a few of the narrow escapes I made today," he noted. "It was a time to test a man's courage."

Few passed the test. One by one, Confederate artillerymen began abandoning their guns and fleeing toward the back of the hill, where they hoped to find cover. It was little safer there. Many Union projectiles skimmed over the crest and exploded beyond, killing men and battery horses alike. So many animals were victims of the shelling that for years afterward the place was known as "Dead Horse Hill."

One man who did not seek safety was Capt. Willie Pegram. With his pale face, wavy hair and thick spectacles, the earnest 21-year-old officer looked more like a graduate student than a warrior, but in his breast beat the heart of a lion. Pegram commanded six of the 14 guns on Prospect Hill. As his men fled their pieces, Pegram shouted at them to return. When they did not obey, he wrapped himself in the battery's flag and strode calmly amongst the deserted guns, as if to shame his men by a display of his own boundless courage.

Capt. James Hall matched Pegram's coolness under fire. Hall commanded one of the Union batteries that were firing at Prospect Hill. He was chatting with some fellow officers when a solid shot skipped past him and struck a nearby ammunition chest. A deafening explosion followed. Nonplussed, Hall walked over to the nearest cannon, sighted it, and sent a shell screeching toward the enemy lines. His shot was right on the mark, detonating a Confederate ammunition chest. Having exacted his revenge, Hall calmly returned to his conversation.

Shots like Hall's had their effect. One by one the Confederate guns fell silent. After an hour Meade determined that the time had come to strike. The 3,800 men of his division rose to their feet and started toward the smoking ridge. As they passed through the line of barking Union guns, a sooty artilleryman shouted after them: "Boys, we have done our duty, now go and do yours."

Mannsfield before the war

Mannsfield

Two miles south of Fredericksburg, overlooking the Rappahannock River, stood Mannsfield, Fredericksburg's most elegant antebellum house. The Georgian-style stone structure was the center of a sprawling 1,800-acre estate. Gracefully curving hyphens connected the main building with its two wings. A long, straight driveway led past a grove of trees to the Richmond Stage Road (modern Route 2/17). Behind the house stood a garden and the family cemetery, while 30 supporting structures — barns, farm offices, slave quarters, etc. — flanked the main building to the north and south.

Mannsfield played a major role as a headquarters and hospital at the Battle of Fredericksburg. The owner at that time was Arthur Bernard, a 50-year-old bachelor worth $150,000. Census records show that Bernard owned at least 77 slaves at the beginning of the Civil War, ranging in age from 70 years to 4 months. He was a strong-headed fellow, and it wasn't long before he put himself on the wrong side of Union authorities. Gen. John F. Reynolds' corps crossed the Rappahannock River one-half mile above Mannsfield on Dec. 12, 1862. When Reynolds' troops marched across Bernard's fields, the outraged owner demanded that the army take another route. Reynolds responded by clapping the Southerner in irons and sending him under arrest to Aquia Landing.

Reynolds proceeded to make Mannsfield his headquarters. He shared the building with at least three other generals: William B. Franklin, William F. "Baldy" Smith and Albion Howe. Although most of the furniture had been removed by the owner earlier in the war, several expensive carpets, fine paintings and gilt candelabras remained. To rough soldiers used to sleeping out of doors in tents or cabins, occupation of the mansion with its warm coal grates was heaven. "It seemed a sin to take possession of so handsome a drawing room," wrote Col. Charles Wainwright, "but we did not injure anything, and as I stretched my blankets on the fine Bruxelles carpet, and looked around at the handsome pictures and bright fire, I for once thanked my stars that I was a staff officer."

Late in the day, Union army commander Ambrose E. Burnside met with Franklin, Reynolds and Smith at *Mannsfield*. After examining the terrain, the generals retired to Arthur Bernard's study to discuss a plan of action for the next day. They agreed to attack the Confederate-held heights south of Fredericksburg. Burnside returned to his headquarters across the river, promising to send written orders later that evening.

While Franklin and his officers waited at Mannsfield for Burnside's orders, soldiers of the Iron Brigade bivouacked outside the house. One

man inadvertently let a sow out of its pen. In its dash to freedom, the agitated animal ran over one of Franklin's staff, who was lying on the ground nearby. The angry officer seized the soldier and had him tied to a tree, where he remained until his regimental commander secured his release.

Other soldiers went to work chopping down trees on the property to use as firewood. A black servant in the 6th Wisconsin regiment at one time had been a slave at Mannsfield. As two soldiers started taking their axes to an old tree, the man became upset. He explained that Bernard's father had planted the tree and that it would break the old man's heart if they cut it down. He urged the soldiers to let the tree stand, but whether they heeded his plea is unknown.

The following day, Union troops attacked the heights. Franklin and the other generals moved their headquarters into the nearby grove so that surgeons could use the house as a field hospital. Gen. George D. Bayard, the 27-year-old commander of Franklin's cavalry, was chatting with a group of officers in the grove when a Confederate cannonball tore through his body, carrying away his thighs, a hip, and part of his abdomen. Bayard stubbornly clung to life. Friends carried him into the house, but doctors could do nothing to save him.

Chaplain E.T. Roe visited the young officer shortly before his death. "Of all the ghastly wounds I saw that day his was the most awful," he remembered. "It needed but a glance to see, as he

calmly stated to those who visited him, 'that his days on earth were numbered.'" Roe was astounded by Bayard's tranquil demeanor. "He talked calmly of his death as of a settled thing, and only inquired particularly how much time he had left on earth." Doctors optimistically predicted that he might live 48 hours, but he died later that night. "My heart sank within me as he gave me his hand in farewell," remembered Roe, "and I almost murmured, 'Why are the best taken?'"

Roe left Bayard's room and walked through the house, which was now packed with wounded and dying men. "Cries and groans resounded from every apartment. Ghastly and bloody wounds met the eye in every direction. Some had their eyes shot out; the tongues of some were swollen out of their mouths; some had their bodies shot through; others were torn and mangled by shell and shot, and all were crowded wherever there was any space." Some soldiers took the chaplain to be a doctor. One asked him to dress a wound; another showed him a hole in his arm and asked if he would have to lose the limb.

Unable to endure such scenes, Roe wandered outside. Night was falling, and he sought shelter in a stone passageway under the house that had been used by Bernard to store tobacco. As he lay his blanket on the cold stone floor he noticed something white lying against the wall. At first he thought it was a dog, but upon closer inspection it proved to be a pile of amputated arms and legs. By then, the jaded clergyman no longer cared. "...I had seen so much of blood and horror during the day that I had grown callous. I quietly spread my blanket within 10 feet of the bloody heap, and listened sadly to the shrieks and groans from the hospital above till I fell asleep."

By the time the Union army retreated across the river two days later, Mannsfield had been vandalized and its grounds had become a graveyard. Northern soldiers seemed to take particular delight in destroying Bernard's fine library. A Confederate soldier visiting the house a few days later found books on the floor, damaged bookcases and bayonet holes through a fine oil painting that hung on the wall. It was enough to "make any book lover's heart ache," he lamented.

Mannsfield did not survive the war. On April 4, 1863, Confederate soldiers who were cooking in the house accidentally set fire to the building and destroyed it. The structure's charred walls remained standing as late as 1891, but in time they too disappeared, their stones being used for other building projects. Today the Elk Lodge No. 875 occupies the site of the historic house.

George D. Bayard

Confederates at Hamilton's Crossing

The Struggle for Prospect Hill

When people think about the Battle of Fredericksburg, they picture the assaults against Marye's Heights, where Confederate soldiers standing behind a stone wall beat back wave after wave of Union attacks. That is the battle's enduring image and rightly so; however, four miles to the south another attack took place, an attack that, if properly supported, might have brought the Union army victory. It was there that the outcome of the battle was decided.

Gen. William B. Franklin directed the Union attacks on the southern end of the battlefield. Opposite him, on a wooded ridge known as Prospect Hill, stood Gen. "Stonewall" Jackson's Confederates. Franklin's goal was to pierce Jackson's line and seize a military road that ran along the crest of the ridge. Once in possession of that road, Franklin could move up the ridge, unraveling the Confederate line like a cheaply knit sweater.

Franklin, however, misinterpreted the orders given to him by his commander, Gen. Ambrose E. Burnside. Instead of attacking Prospect Hill with a large force, he committed just two divisions — just one-third of his command. Gen. George G. Meade's Pennsylvania division spearheaded the assault, supported on his right by the troops of Gen. John Gibbon.

Meade deployed his 3,800-man division in the fields adjacent to the Richmond Stage Road (modern Route 2/17), near the spot now occupied by the General Motors Powertrain plant. To reach the heights, his men would have to cross one-half mile of open ground, cross the Richmond, Fredericksburg, and Potomac Railroad (now CSX), then charge up the hill and into the woods.

A Confederate artilleryman, watching the buildup of Union troops on the plain below, thought that enemy host might "eat us up," but Jackson had no such concern. Earlier in the day, when a staff officer had expressed doubt that the Confederates could defeat the thousands of Union soldiers arrayed against them, Jackson brushed aside his fears. "Major, my men may sometimes fail to take a position, but to defend one, never! I am glad the Yankees are coming!"

Jackson had good reason to be confident. At Fredericksburg he had nearly 40,000 troops to meet Meade's attack — more than four men for every linear foot of ground he defended. A.P. Hill's division held the front line, near the railroad. Behind Hill, stacked upon one another like layers in a club sandwich, were the remaining three divisions of Jackson's corps. Fredericksburg was the only battle in which Jackson could boast an abundance of troops. He would need most of them before the day ended.

At 1 p.m., following a heavy artillery bombardment, the Union line started forward. Meade directed his attack toward a small ribbon of trees that extended east beyond the railroad. The ground there was marshy, and Hill had left it undefended, thinking it impassable by attacking troops. It was not. As Confederate skirmishers gave way, Meade's men drove across the railroad embankment, slogged through the muddy ground and charged up the slope beyond.

As they approached the top of the ridge, they crashed headlong into Maxcy Gregg's South Carolina brigade, which Hill had placed in reserve immediately behind the gap. Gregg was an uncompromising proponent of states' rights and an ardent supporter of secession. As commander of the South Carolina's 1st Infantry Regiment, he

had taken part in the bombardment of Fort Sumter and gloried in its capture. Now, as an experienced brigadier general, he found himself squarely in the path of Meade's thrust.

Hill gave Gregg the task of covering the gap in his line. Hill did not think the Union army would attack the swampy interval, but if it did, Gregg was to engage the Federals in front while brigades on either side of the gap gnawed at the attackers' flanks. Meade's assault, however, caught Gregg unawares. It appears that the Southern general — who was stone deaf — either didn't hear Hill's order to fill the gap or didn't appreciate that the fighting had started. As the Pennsylvanians swarmed through the woods, they found Gregg's men eating dinner, their rifles stacked neatly in the military road.

Some of the South Carolinians, seeing the Union line approaching, grabbed their guns and began firing. Fearful that his men were targeting their own skirmishers, Gregg rode down the line and ordered his men to stop shooting. Too late he realized that the soldiers coming up the hill were indeed the enemy. The Confederate skirmishers on Gregg's front had retreated by a different route.

Before Gregg could rectify his mistake, a bullet pierced his spine, inflicting a mortal wound. Moments later Union troops charged through his brigade, scattering it to the winds. Against all odds, Meade's division had broken Jackson's line and seized the military road! But it was one thing to seize a position; it was another thing to hold it.

Union troops attack Prospect Hill

Meade had just 3,800 men; Jackson had nearly 40,000. If Meade was going to maintain his grip on the hill, he needed help and fast. To his astonishment, he discovered that no reinforcements were at hand. Gen. Franklin, interpreting his orders as a reconnaissance-in-force rather than a general assault, had kept most of his troops back at the pontoon bridges, two miles away. Meade was on his own.

Before help could reach him, the Confederates launched a massive counterattack. From its position in the rear of Hill's line, Gen. Jubal A. Early's division came crashing through the trees, screaming the rebel yell. Farther north, the troops of Gen. William Taliaferro's division also joined the fray. Hit on all sides by an overwhelming force, Meade's tired and disorganized division burst like a bubble. The general tried to rally his troops along the railroad embankment, but the line simply would not hold. The defeated bluecoats tumbled out of the woods and streamed back across the plain toward the

Maxcy Gregg

Richmond Stage Road.

Content to have reestablished their line, most Confederates halted at the railroad. One impetuous Georgia brigade, however, pursued the Union army onto the plain. It was a costly mistake. Caught in the open, without cover, the Georgians were stopped dead in their tracks by Meade's artillery and fell back with heavy losses. By 2:30 p.m., both sides were back where they started.

Meade was furious. His troops had punched a hole in Jackson's line and seized the military road against overwhelming odds only to relinquish their gains for lack of proper support. In the process, they had lost 1,850 men killed, wounded or captured — nearly half of those who had taken part in the attack. Meade himself narrowly escaped death when a bullet pierced his hat. But it was all for naught. As a result of the bad communication between Burnside and Franklin, the Union army had lost its best chance for victory.

The Fighting at Bernard's Cabins

Halfway down Lee Drive, a little more than a half mile beyond its intersection with Lansdowne Road, begins one of the newest and least known trails on the Fredericksburg Battlefield. The trail starts at the road and winds through the woods for half a mile before emerging into a large ploughed field overlooking Shannon Airport and the Richmond, Fredericksburg, and Potomac Railroad (now CSX). It terminates at Bernard's Cabins, the site of a small slave community. The cabins and their occupants belonged to Arthur Bernard, the owner of Mannsfield, a plantation house that stood about one and a half miles to the east.

During the Battle of Fredericksburg, Bernard's Cabins became an important Confederate artillery position on Stonewall Jackson's end of the line. Jackson held nearly a two-mile front along the R.F.&P. Railroad. The center of his line was wooded, preventing the Confederate leader from placing any artillery there. Instead, he placed a large number of cannons on either side of the woods and angled the guns toward one another so as to catch Union troops who might attempt to attack the woods in a deadly crossfire.

To the right of the woods Jackson had Lt. Col. Rueben Lindsey Walker's battalion of 14 guns. To the left of the woods, at Bernard's Cab-ins, stood nine guns of Capt. Greenlee Davidson's battalion. Jackson determined that Davidson's guns were too far back to cover the woods on his right effectively. Before the fighting began he sent Capt. John B. Brockenbrough forward with 12 additional guns to take position on Davidson's right-front, beyond the railroad tracks. Brockenbrough's position placed him directly in front of Gen. James Lane's North Carolina brigade and immediately to the left of a marshy gap in Jackson's line.

On the morning of Dec. 13, 1862, Union skirmishers crept forward through the mist-shrouded fields and began shooting at Brockenbrough's exposed gunners. When Lane's men were unable to drive them away, Brockenbrough opened on the pesky Union riflemen with canister: large cylinders filled with dozens of marble-sized iron balls that had the effect of a giant shotgun blast. Brockenbrough's guns drew the fire of Union artillery batteries on the plain ahead. Soon the Confederate guns were under an intense fire from enemy sharpshooters and cannon alike. Brockenbrough fell with a crippling wound to the arm, and one of his battery commanders was struck in the thigh. With casualties mounting, the battered battalion withdrew from its exposed position east of the railroad and fell back behind

Davidson's guns to the safety of the woods.

Convinced that he had silenced most of the enemy cannons, Union Gen. George G. Meade ordered his division to attack the heights. Supporting Meade, on the right, was Gen. John Gibbon's division. Altogether the two divisions numbered approximately 7,800 men. Meade's division had the good fortune to find a 600-yard hole in Jackson's line. Pushing through the gap, it routed a South Carolina brigade and seized a military road that ran along the crest of the hill.

John Gibbon

Gibbon found the going tougher. The 35-year-old Pennsylvanian steered his division toward the woods on Meade's right. His course brought him into direct collision with Lane's North Carolinians, who held a strong position behind the railroad embankment. Lane initially held his own, repulsing attacks by two of Gibbon's three brigades. But as Meade's men poured through the gap and begin filtering into the woods on Lane's right flank, the North Carolina line began to unravel. Sensing victory, Gibbon's men surged forward for a third time. Cascading down the slope and over the railroad embankment, they engaged Lane's men in hand-to-hand combat. One hundred and eighty Confederates threw down their arms in surrender; the rest fell back through the woods and formed a new line 100 yards to the rear.

Having seized the railroad, Union soldiers made a dash for Davidson's nine guns, now just a few hundred yards away. The North Carolina captain waited until the Federals were within easy range, then let loose with a deadly storm of canister. "The head of the column went down like wheat before the reaper," he wrote with satisfaction. "Another and another volley in quick succession completed the work. The Yankees broke, took to their heels and you never saw such a stampede in your life." The slave cabins and a small pine grove had stood between Davidson and his Yankee assailants, but no more. By the time he

stopped shooting, the cabins were in ruins and the grove had been reduced to kindling.

Gibbon reformed his division along the captured railroad. By then, he was under pressure from all sides. On the left, Meade's division had given way, exposing Gibbon's flank to attack. In the center, Lane's brigade — heavily reinforced — was pushing forward in an effort to retake the railroad. On the right, Davidson's guns continued to pour shot and shell into the ragged Union line. When Gibbon had to leave the field with an injured hand, his successor, Gen. Nelson Taylor, wisely ordered a retreat. Jackson had repaired the break in his line.

Gen. William B. Franklin was in overall command of the Union troops below Fredericksburg. No sooner had Meade's and Gibbon's men returned to their starting point on the Richmond Stage Road (modern Route 2/17), than Union commander Ambrose E. Burnside ordered Franklin to renew the attacks. Franklin said that he would try, but it was a hollow promise. He had no stomach for frontal assaults, and with his grand division beaten and bloody, his only concern was maintaining a line of retreat.

Jackson was not so timid. Not content to simply repulse Franklin's attacks, he planned a crushing counterstroke that would drive the Union army into the Rappahannock River. At sunset, his artillery rolled forward in an effort to soften up the Union position for the attack. Franklin's guns responded with a vengeance. At Bernard's Cabins, Union shot ignited one of Davidson's ammunition chests. Fifteen or 20 shells caught fire and exploded, blackening the ground and stampeding the battery horses. One shell cut a Confederate gunner in two and threw his charred clothing into a nearby tree; another took off the leg of an officer just above the knee. Jackson witnessed the vigor of the Union response and wisely cancelled the attack. South of Fredericksburg, the battle was over.

View up Hanover Street toward Marye's Heights

Edwin Sumner Begins His Assault

Behind the Fredericksburg Battlefield Visitor Center on Lafayette Boulevard is a 40-foot-high ridge known as Marye's Heights. This modest acclivity was the focal point of repeated brave but fruitless Union assaults on Dec. 13, 1862. Confederate forces commanded by Gen. James Longstreet occupied the ridge. Nine guns of the Washington Artillery, a crack unit from New Orleans, La., held the crest, while a Georgia infantry brigade — perhaps 1,000 men — occupied a sunken road that ran along its base. Another 3,000 North Carolinians were on hand near by, ready to reinforce the Georgians in the sunken road if needed.

At first glance the position did not seem all that formidable, but looks can be deceiving. Marye's Heights was, in fact, a fortress — the strongest natural defensive position enjoyed by Gen. Robert E. Lee's Army of Northern Virginia during the war. It was high enough to allow Confederate artillerymen on the crest to fire over the heads of their comrades in the road below, yet low enough to allow the gunners to scour the fields in front. The Georgians, by like token, found a ready-made trench in the sunken road and the 4-foot-high stone wall that bordered it.

Union troops attacking Marye's Heights had no such advantages. Fredericksburg then hugged the Rappahannock River, extending west only four blocks, to Prince Edward Street. Between the town and the ridge was open ground, offering little in the way of protective cover. To make matters worse, a millrace carrying excess water away from the Fredericksburg canal circumscribed the town like a belt before emptying into the river near the train depot. The canal ditch, which later was paved to form Kenmore Avenue, was approximately 15 feet wide and 6 feet deep. To cross it, Union troops would have to break ranks, splash through the cold water, clamber up the muddy bank on the opposite side, and reform — all under the searching fire of Confederate artillery on the ridge.

The task of capturing Marye's Heights fell to Gen. Edwin V. Sumner, the commander of Burnside's Right Grand Division. At age 65, Sumner was the oldest active corps commander in the Union army. His military service stretched back more than four decades, to the year 1819, before most men in the Army of the Potomac — including its commander, Ambrose E. Burnside — were even born. Sumner was well liked by his troops, who had nicknamed him "Bull Head" (or simply "Bull") after a spent bullet reputedly ricocheted off his head doing him no harm. Beneath his long gray locks and dignified demeanor, beat the heart of a brave and faithful soldier. In an army known for its jealousies and intrigues, Sumner stood out for his honesty and devotion to the Union. Some might question his ability, but none could question the old soldier's courage or his fidelity to the cause.

At Fredericksburg, Sumner commanded the Second and Ninth corps, together numbering nearly 30,000 men. Because of the terrain, he had to attack across a narrow front. Rather than throw his entire force against the ridge in one grand assault, as Lee would later do at Gettysburg, Sumner had to feed his brigades into the battle one or two at a time. From the air the blue lines, advancing in regular intervals of 200 yards, would have looked like waves lapping against the shore.

Gen. Nathan Kimball's brigade led the assault. Known as the "Gibraltar Brigade," Kimball's command included two new regiments, which never had tasted combat. Fredericksburg would be their baptism of fire. Kimball led his troops across the millrace near the train depot and deployed them in line of battle on the plain beyond, near modern Lee Avenue. As he did so, a fog that had blanketed the town began to clear, exposing his brigade to Confederate guns on Marye's Heights. Solid shot began to rain down on the Union soldiers, knocking some of them out of the ranks. Kimball galloped to the front of the brigade in an effort to encourage his terrified men. "Cheer up, my hearties, cheer up!" he cried. "This is something we must all get used to! Remember, this brigade has never been whipped — don't let it get whipped today!" In a less inspired moment, the general told a regiment, "Look out boys, they can't kill all of you, but they may hurt some of you." His men found cold comfort in that assurance.

It was almost noon when Kimball finally led his men across the deadly plain. Fragments of Confederate artillery shells pelted the advancing Union line, creating too many holes for the officers to fill. When the Gibraltar Brigade got within 200 yards of the heights, the Georgia riflemen in the road let loose a devastating volley that injured Kimball and nearly annihilated his brigade. Union survivors fled back toward the town or sought

shelter in a shallow ravine approximately 150 yards from the stone wall. It was a grim pattern that would be repeated more than a dozen times that afternoon. By 2 p.m., the bodies of more than 5,000 Union soldiers littered the plain in front of Marye's Heights. Sumner had committed 10 brigades to the attack, but not one had reached the sunken road. His grand division was a wreck.

Gen. Darius Couch watched the slaughter from his vantage point in the courthouse cupola. What he witnessed through the smoky haze

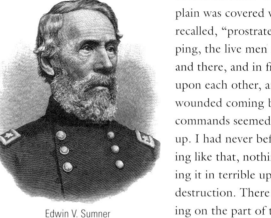
Edwin V. Sumner

chilled his soul. "...The whole plain was covered with men," he recalled, "prostrate and dropping, the live men running here and there, and in front closing upon each other, and the wounded coming back. The commands seemed to be mixed up. I had never before seen fighting like that, nothing approaching it in terrible uproar and destruction. There was no cheering on the part of the men, but a stubborn determination to obey orders and do their duty." One by one, he remembered sadly, each new brigade approached the wall only to dissolve "like snow coming down on warm ground." By now, it was clear that Marye's Heights could not be taken by frontal assault. Committing more men to the attack would only increase the casualties. "It is only murder now," Couch informed his superiors.

But Burnside refused to listen. The Union commander was monitoring the progress of the battle from his command post at the Phillips house, two miles behind the front. The lack of success in both Franklin's and Sumner's sectors frustrated, but did not daunt, him. At the Antietam he had been criticized for a lack of aggression; he would not make the same mistake at Fredericksburg. At 2:30 p.m. Burnside ordered Franklin to renew his assault south of town and instructed Gen. Joseph Hooker, commanding the army's reserves, to support Sumner's attack on Marye's Heights. The carnage would continue.

The Battle of Fredericksburg

Confederates on the sunken road

Tom Cobb Gives His Life for the Confederacy

Among those who fought for the Confederacy, few were more brilliant — or more querulous — than Gen. Thomas Reade Rootes Cobb. Few also would have a more important role in the Battle of Fredericksburg. Cobb was born in 1823 at "Cherry Hill," his family's Georgia plantation, where he reputedly weighed in at a whopping 21.5 pounds! After graduating first in his class at the University of Georgia, Cobb embarked on a legal career. Over the next 18 years he produced a number of important treatises on Georgia law, including several monographs defending slavery. Not surprisingly, Cobb later played a leading role in the secessionist movement. He was a delegate to the convention that took Georgia out of the Union, and when Georgia banded together with other seceding states to form the Southern Confederacy, Cobb became a member of the new nation's Provisional Congress.

Cobb was not content with simply being a legislator, however, and in 1861 he raised a heterogeneous unit composed of infantry, artillery and cavalry, which came to be known as Cobb's Legion. Despite the fact that he had no military experience, the politician-turned-warrior took the field as the legion's colonel. Cobb's older brother, Howell, had followed a similar path and in 1862 commanded a brigade in Robert E. Lee's Army of Northern Virginia. When Howell transferred to a different military theater in November of that year, Lee promoted to Tom Cobb to brigadier general and assigned him command of his brother's old brigade.

Cobb achieved brigade command despite a contentious personality and a mercurial temper. He found fault with just about everything and everybody, including Jefferson Davis and Robert E. Lee. He accused Davis of "malignant persecution" for trying to break up his legion (which was a very sensible measure from a military standpoint) and criticized Lee as being "haughty and boorish and supercilious in his bearing…particularly so to me." Cobb's self-righteous petulance gained him few friends and many enemies. His troops considered him strict and overbearing, so much so that one man later claimed to have purposely fired the shot that killed Cobb at Fredericksburg. Although the story is patently false, it demonstrates the strong dislike many men had toward their newly minted general.

The Confederate army reached Fredericksburg in late November 1862. Cobb's brigade initially took a position near Howison Hill (now adjacent to the park tour road, Lee Drive, one half mile south of Lafayette Boulevard). Cobb recognized the

Thomas R.R. Cobb

strength of the position and hoped ardently that the Federals would be foolish enough to attack it. "I think my Brigade can whip ten thousand of them attacking us in front," he wrote prophetically. "We have a magnificent position, the best perhaps on the line." Cobb's only regret was that a Union crossing near Fredericksburg would lead inevitably to the destruction of the town. "If they attempt it," he wrote his wife, "poor old Fredericksburg is a doomed city and will be reduced to ashes as we shall be forced to destroy it before leaving it in their hands." Cobb had a strong affection for Fredericksburg, for his mother, Sarah Rootes, had grown up at "Federal Hill," a house on the outskirts of the town. The thought that Yankees might despoil or destroy his mother's home so infuriated Cobb that he advised Lee "to raise the black flag and give no quarter to any scoundrel that crosses the river."

As weeks passed without any movement on the part of the Union army, Cobb began to lose hope that the enemy would cross the river before spring. As late as Dec. 10 he told his wife that he did not anticipate a battle at Fredericksburg, at least not in the near future. Instead, he thought the Federals would spend the winter gathering their strength for a major effort in the spring. Re-

gardless of what happened, the impetuous general promised his wife that he would take care of himself. "Do not be uneasy about my being 'rash,'" he told her. "The bubble of reputation cannot drag me into folly. God helping me, I hope to do my duty when called upon, trusting the consequences to Him."

The day after Cobb wrote this letter the Union army began laying pontoon bridges opposite Fredericksburg. The following day, Dec. 12, thousands of Union soldiers poured across the river and occupied the town. The battle for which Cobb had yearned finally had arrived. At the orders of his superior, Gen. Lafayette McLaws, Cobb moved his brigade up to Marye's Heights, occupying a sunken road that ran along the foot of the ridge. A 4-foot-tall stone wall that bordered the lane provided Cobb's Georgians with a stout, ready-made trench.

Shortly before noon, Dec. 13, the Union army deployed in front of Marye's Heights with the evident intention of attacking Cobb's line. The general wanted to thrash the Yankee hordes to prove that he deserved his recent promotion. It was with disdain, therefore, that he received a note from McLaws ordering him to fall back should the troops on his left be unable to hold their position. "Well!" Cobb sniffed, "if they wait for me to fall back, they will wait a long time." The Georgian was there to stay.

The Union attacks began around noon. As the first blue line started forward, Cobb waved his hat in the air and shouted, "Get ready, boys, here they come!" When the Federals reached a point 200 yards from the wall, the Georgians let loose a wicked volley. When the smoke cleared, the Union line had virtually disappeared, annihilated by the fire of Cobb's men. Other attacks would follow. In

The Battle of Fredericksburg

between, the Union army pounded Marye's Heights with artillery.

Cobb was standing in the road, adjacent to his head-quarters at the Stephens house, when a Union shell came crashing through the building. As it exited, the shell exploded, wounding Cobb and killing two others. A piece of shrapnel sliced through the general's left thigh, smashing the bone and severing the femoral artery. Blood spilled onto the dirt road. Members of Cobb's staff fashioned a tourniquet in an effort to stanch the flow then carried him down the Telegraph Road (modern Lafayette Boulevard) to a field hospital in the rear. As he left the field, the dying officer cried out, "I am only wounded, boys, hold your ground like brave men." Cobb was treated at the Wiet house, located near modern Spotswood Baptist Church. Doctors struggled to save the general's life, but his injury was too severe. At 2 p.m., wrote Cobb's friend, Chaplain R.K. Porter, "the glorious light went out forever."

The Cobb Monument

Irish Brigade soldiers

The Irish Brigade

Of the many Union charges at Fredericksburg, by far the most celebrated was that of the Irish Brigade.

Gaelic immigrants, who had come to America in the 1840s and '50s to escape famine and political turmoil in their home country, comprised the brigade. Their leader was Gen. Thomas Francis Meagher (pronounced Marr), a 39-year-old Irish nationalist who had been arrested for fomenting rebellion against the British government and exiled to Tasmania, an island halfway around the world. Meagher managed to escape his island prison after three years and fled to the United States, settling in New York City. He rose to become a leading spokesman for the Irish-American community, and when the Civil War began he rallied his countrymen to support the Union cause. "Every blow you strike in the cause of the Union," he told his volunteers, "is aimed at the allies of England, the enemy of your land and race. Today it is for the American Republic we fight — tomorrow it will be for Ireland."

In February 1862 President Abraham Lincoln authorized Meagher to organize a brigade of Irish immigrants culled from cities in the Northeast. Initially the unit had just three regiments — the 63rd, 69th and 88th New York — but the addition of the 28th Massachusetts and 116th Pennsylvania later in the year brought the brigade up to full strength. By December 1862, it numbered 1,200 rifles.

To remind his men of their heritage, Meagher had each regiment carry a green flag bearing the golden harp of Ireland. (The one exception was the 116th Pennsylvania, which was not fully Irish.) The flags of the older regiments had been badly shot up in earlier campaigns, however, and a few days before the Battle of Fredericksburg Meagher sent them back north to be replaced by new flags. Before the replacement banners arrived, the army crossed the Rappahannock River. Consequently, the only regiment that carried the Irish colors into battle at Fredericksburg was the 28th Massachusetts.

Meagher and his brigade entered Fredericksburg on Dec. 12, making camp at the steamboat landing at the lower end of town (the modern city dock). The troops carried three days' rations and 60 rounds of ammunition. Stacking arms, they dispersed to explore the town. Many took part in the shameless pillaging that followed, despite denials of their commander to the contrary. By evening they returned to the landing and bedded down in the cold mud to spend what, for many, would be their last night on earth.

Before dawn the shrill call of the bugle brought the men to their feet. They made themselves a hasty breakfast of coffee, pork and hardtack before forming ranks and moving up to the railroad. Around noon the battle began, and Confederate cannonballs crashed through the buildings around them. "It was a time well calculated to try the stoutest hearts," remembered one soldier. Casualties from other units came drifting back from the front. A shell had sliced through the leg of one soldier, and it dangled from his body by a piece of flesh. He begged those carrying him to sever the mangled limb, but they were too intent on getting to the rear to stop. A man in the 116th Pennsylvania drew a knife and mercifully removed the useless appendage.

After a two-hour wait, the Irish Brigade moved up Caroline Street to George Street. The battle was in full swing now, and Confederate projectiles rained down on the unit with increasing venom. The bombardment clearly put the troops on edge. To steady them, Meagher ordered the men to place sprigs of boxwood in their caps. The greenery, he explained, would remind the troops of their Irish heritage. The general then addressed each regiment, urging it to do its duty and strike a deadly blow to the traitors of its country. "This may be my last speech to you," he told one unit, "but I will be with you when the battle is the fiercest; and, if I fall, I can say I did my duty, and fell fighting in the most glorious of causes." The brigade responded with three cheers.

It was then about 12:30 p.m. Four Union brigades had attacked Marye's Heights and failed; it was now the Irish Brigade's turn to enter the fray. At the command, "Shoulder arms, right face, forward, double quick, march!" Meagher's men turned up George Street and headed through town toward the dreaded ridge. As they crested the hill, Confederate artillery opened on the brigade with renewed violence. Shells exploded overhead, while solid shot caromed down the lane, ricocheting off buildings and knocking soldiers from the ranks. One particularly deadly shell exploded in the midst of the 88th New York, injuring 18 men. The brigade broke into a trot as it descended the shallow valley behind modern Maury School. At the bottom of the hill a canal ditch blocked its path. (After the war this canal ditch was filled in to form Kenmore Avenue.) The soldiers broke ranks, splashed through the muddy obstruction, and reformed ranks on the other side, in the shadow of a slight ridge. An officer remembered those harrowing moments: "In a few minutes came the word, 'Attention!' and every man was upon his feet again; then 'Fix Bayonets!' and as this was being done, the clink, clink of the cold steel sounding along the line made one's blood run cold."

Thomas F. Meagher

After what seemed an eternity, Meagher gave the order, "Irish Brigade advance. Forward, double quick; guide center." With a shout the brigade rose to its feet and charged over the hill and across the plain leading to Marye's Heights. A hail of musketry greeted the five regiments as they left the cover of the valley. "Officers and men fell in rapid succession," wrote Lt. Col. St. Clair Mulholland of the 116th Pennsylvania Volunteers. "Lieutenant Garrett Nowlen...fell with a ball through the thigh. Major Bardwell fell badly wounded; and a ball whistled through Lieutenant Bob McGuire's lungs. Lieutenant Christian Foltz fell dead, with a ball through the brain. The orderly sergeant of Company H wheeled around, gazed upon Lieutenant Quinlan, and a great stream of blood poured from a hole in his forehead...." Ignoring its losses, the brigade pressed on toward the ridge, the men dropping by scores. "No cheers or wild hurrahs as they moved towards the foe," remembered Mulholland. "They were not there to fight, only to die."

Irish Brigade drum

The unit advanced to within 50 yards of the rebel line. By then all organization was gone. Most of the regimental officers had been shot, and many companies had lost half their men. The brigade stood its ground for a few minutes, exchanging fire with the Confederates, then dissolved into the broken, bleeding sea of humanity lying at the foot of the heights. Some soldiers ran the gauntlet of fire back to town; others stayed at the front until sunset then retreated under the cover of darkness.

The next morning just 230 men of the brigade rallied to the colors. Several hundred others straggled in during the course of the day, but nearly half the brigade lay bleeding in front of Marye's Heights. In the final tally, the Irish Brigade lost 545 men at Fredericksburg, 45 percent of the men it took into the battle, including 14 of its 15 field officers. The only officer above the rank of captain to escape harm was Col. Patrick Kelly of the 88th New York. He narrowly cheated death when a bullet pierced his coat just below his spine. Yet terrible as the Irish Brigade's toll was, it did not match the casualties suffered by Gen. John C. Caldwell's brigade, which followed it into battle. Caldwell lost a staggering 952 men.

Today a monument to the Irish Brigade stands at the city dock, where the brigade bivouacked prior to the battle. In addition, the drum of the 28th Massachusetts Volunteers is on display at the Fredericksburg Battlefield Visitor Center. These objects remind us of the exemplary courage shown by the Irish Brigade and indeed by every Union brigade that charged Marye's Heights that day.

Confederate artillerymen on Marye's Heights

The Washington Artillery Defends Marye's Heights

Artillery played an important role on many Civil War battlefields, but it rarely had a more decisive result than at Fredericksburg, where Confederate guns broke up repeated Union assaults and inflicted thousands of casualties. Gen. Ambrose E. Burnside's delay in crossing the Rappahannock River had given Southern engineers three weeks to prepare for the attacks. On Marye's Heights, directly behind the town, they had constructed more than half a dozen U-shaped gun pits to protect Confederate artillerymen from hostile fire. Col. Edward Porter Alexander ordered the engineers to build the gun pits along the brow of the hill so that Confederate cannon could sweep the plain in front. Later, when Gen. Robert E. Lee inspected the works, he criticized Alexander for building the pits along the brow of the hill rather than back on its crest. Alexander held his ground, however, and as a result the Confederate guns inflicted appalling damage on the attacking Union columns. The young officer could not pass up the chance to let his commander know that he had been right. A few days after the battle, within Lee's hearing, Alexander remarked to a fellow officer how fortunate it was that they had kept the guns where they were rather than moving them as Lee had suggested. "I was half afraid the general might think me impertinent," Alexander confessed, "though I could not resist the temptation to take one little dig at him." Lee said nothing, and in the future he often assigned the young officer the task of locating Confederate batteries.

Col. James B. Walton had the task of defending the gun pits that Alexander and the engineers had constructed. A New Jersey native, Walton had attended college in Louisiana and later settled there, opening a grocery store in New Orleans. At Fredericksburg he commanded a battalion of 16 guns known as the Washington Artillery. Walton's men reached Fredericksburg in mid-November to find the Union army still across the Rappahannock River in Stafford County. With little to do, the Confederates made camp and relaxed. Some paid visits to acquaintances in town, others put on a theatrical production, but most simply bided their time thinking of home.

The Union army put an end to their reveries. On Dec. 11, 1862, the Army of the Potomac crossed the river and took possession of Fredericksburg. The booming of two signal guns at

Sandy Bottom

5 a.m. gave notice of the crossing. Within minutes the Louisianians had hitched up their horses and were moving toward the heights. Walton took possession of the Marye house, Brompton, near the center of the ridge, while his men muscled nine of their 16 guns into the crescent-shaped pits prepared for them earlier by Alexander and the engineers.

Walton's men did not find the gun pits to their liking. The engineers purposely had left the walls low so that the artillerymen could fire over them. Low walls meant less protection. As soon as they reached Marye's Heights, Walton's men increased the height of the works, cutting an opening in the front walls through which the cannons could fire. The engineers complained that the artillerymen had ruined the gun pits, but Walton's men paid them no heed. "We have to fight here, not you; we will arrange them to suit ourselves," they argued. Gen. James Longstreet agreed with the artillerymen, commenting that the extra digging would be well worth the effort if it saved the finger of just one man.

Longstreet had responsibility for defending the left half of the Confederate line, including Marye's Heights. He took his responsibility seriously. When he saw a cannon lying idle, Longstreet suggested that Alexander roll it into position beside Walton's guns. Alexander balked at the idea. "General," he replied, "we cover that ground now so well that we will comb it as with a

fine-tooth comb. A chicken could not live on that field when we open on it." The young artillery officer knew what he was talking about, as later events would show.

The battle took place on Dec. 13. That morning, before the fog lifted, Walton left Brompton and rode across the ridge on his coal-black stallion, Rebel. As he scanned the fields below with his binoculars, he looked, said one man, like "the picture of Napoleon...." Walton found his men awake and ready for action. They had taken the ammunition chests off of the wheeled limbers and placed them on the ground near the guns, allowing the horses and limbers to be sent safely to the rear.

At noon the fog cleared, and Gen. Nathan Kimball's Union brigade started forward shouting "Hi! Hi! Hi!" "It was 12:30 P.M.," wrote Confederate Adjutant William Miller Owen, "and it was evident that we were now going to have it hot and heavy." The Union army deployed on the plain below Marye's Heights and after dressing ranks started forward. "How beautifully they came on!" wrote Owen in admiration. "Their bright bayonets glistening in the sunlight made the line look like a huge serpent of blue and steel."

No sooner did Kimball's line emerge from the cover of the town than Walton's guns opened on them with a savage fury. "We could see our shells bursting in their ranks, making great gaps," re-

The Battle of Fredericksburg

membered Owen, "but on they came, as though they would go straight through and over us." As the blue line surged closer, Confederate gunners switched from shell to canister. Canister consisted of several dozen marble-sized iron balls wrapped in a light metal casing. As the cannon fired, the casing would tear apart, spraying the iron balls in an ever-widening swath of destruction. It had the effect of a large and very deadly shotgun blast.

The canister rounds staggered the Union attackers, but they continued to press forward until hit by the rifle fire of Georgia infantrymen posted in a road at the foot of the hill. Riddled by artillery fire from the heights above and by infantry fire from the road below, some of Kimball's men broke ranks and fled back to town. Others took shelter in a shallow ravine 150 yards from the Confederate line. From there they maintained a steady fire against the artillerymen on the ridge. (This line ran just east of modern Littlepage Street.)

Despite the protection afforded by Alexander's gun pits, Confederate gunners began to go down. "Corporal Ruggles fell mortally wounded," recorded Owen, "and Perry, who seized the rammer as it fell from Ruggles's hand, received a bullet in the arm. Rodd was holding 'vent,' and away went his 'crazy bone.' In quick succession Everett, Rossiter, and Kursheedt were wounded. Falconer in passing in rear of the guns was struck behind the ear and fell dead." So many men were killed or wounded that Walton had to impress nearby infantry troops to help man his guns. Ammunition was harder to replace. As their supply of shell, case shot, and canister ran low, the Washington Artillery had to relinquish its position and go to the rear. Another battalion would have the honor of finishing the fight.

Although the Washington Artillery would take part in dozens of other fights before the war's end, nowhere did it contribute more to Confederate victory than at Fredericksburg. Today cannon still stand on Marye's Heights to remind us of the pivotal role that the Louisianans played in shaping the outcome of the battle.

Shattered limber and caisson behind Marye's Heights, May 1863

Balloon on the ground near Phillips house

Professor Lowe's Observation Balloons

The Civil War has been called the first modern American war. It featured the first successful submarine attack, the first battle between ironclad warships, and the first use of railroads for military purposes. It was also the first war that utilized aerial observation.

The use of balloons for military purposes was the inspiration of a New Hampshire aeronaut named Thaddeus Sobieski Constantine Lowe. Lowe became fascinated with aeronautics as a boy and in 1858, at the age of 26, he constructed a balloon and made his first ascent. His feat fired the popular imagination, and for several months Lowe traveled throughout the country staging exhibitions.

Lowe made his balloons of silk coated with a concoction of linseed oil. It took five seamstresses and 1,200 yards of silk to make the "envelope" that contained the 15,000 cubic feet of hydrogen necessary to lift the balloon. A mesh pouch made of rope encompassed the envelope and supported the basket, or gondola, below.

Lowe was a man with grand ideas, and it wasn't long before he determined to sail his balloon across the Atlantic Ocean. Equipment problems thwarted his efforts (and probably saved his life), however, and he limited his flights to North America. His greatest journey occurred in April 1861. In just nine hours he sailed 900 miles, from Cincinnati, Ohio, to a point near Unionville, S.C. The Civil War had started just one week earlier with the bombardment of Fort Sumter, and when South Carolina farmers saw Lowe's balloon descending in their fields, they suspected a Yankee trick. Lowe was arrested as a spy and taken to the state capital at Columbia. Officials questioned the errant aeronaut, determined that he was harmless, and ordered his release.

In retrospect, they should have confined him. No sooner was Lowe released than he proceeded to Washington to offer his services to President Abraham Lincoln. The president grasped the potential military benefits of aerial observation, and in August he appointed "Professor Lowe" chief of army aeronautics. No military rank came with the title, but Lowe did get a colonel's pay.

Over the next several months the professor conducted aerial observations throughout northern Virginia. When Gen. George B. McClellan took the Army of the Potomac to Fort Monroe for the Peninsula Campaign in the spring of 1862, Lowe accompanied it there. (The Peninsula is the

Professor Lowe in his balloon

neck of land between the James and York Rivers, east of Richmond.) Throughout the campaign, Lowe provided McClellan with important information about the location and movement of Confederate troops.

Observation balloons, however, had their limitations. Before each ascent the envelopes had to be filled with hydrogen. This meant that the balloons could not travel far from a gas works.

Lowe overcame this problem by creating a portable generator capable of producing hydrogen in the field. He designed the generator to fit in the back of a standard army wagon.

Other problems were not so easily overcome. First, there was the weather. Observation balloons could be used only on calm, clear days. Anything more than a gentle wind would buffet the balloon, driving it to ground. Second was the problem of transmitting messages from the balloon to the ground. Lowe experimented using a telegraph, but the tugging of the wires that connected his machine with the one on the ground led to frequent malfunctions. Resorting to a more primitive approach, the professor simply wrote messages on a piece of paper, tied the paper to a rock, and dropped it to the ground. This worked well if you could find the rock, though it was somewhat hazardous to those standing below.

A final problem involved gathering useful information. Lowe and his assistants knew a great deal about aeronautics, but they knew very little about military matters. Their observations were therefore of limited use. To make the most of the balloons, trained military observers had to go aloft. The task usually fell to generals and their staffs.

Fitz John Porter was among the first and only Union generals to make an ascent. While on the Peninsula, he nearly lost his life when a cable snapped, causing his balloon to sail toward enemy lines. Porter tried to bring it back to earth by releasing some of the hydrogen. To reach the vent, however, he had to lean out of the gondola. In doing so, he nearly fell out. To make matters worse, Confederate artillery fired on the wayward craft. Although Porter survived the incident, it's doubtful whether he ever hazarded another ascent.

At the Battle of Fredericksburg, responsibility for making aerial observations fell to Lt. Col. William Teall, an officer on Gen. Edwin Sumner's staff. Sumner himself refused to go up, considering the trip a risk "greater than marching in front of the cannon's mouth." (He probably had heard about Porter's experience.) Lowe's balloon, *Eagle*, made four ascents during the battle, and Teall was on three of them.

At Fredericksburg, however, the balloon was of little value. On the first three ascents, it was too windy for Teall make accurate observations. The fourth ascent was more profitable. By then the winds had died down, and the *Eagle* ascended 800 to 900 feet in the air, offering the staffer a breathtaking glimpse of the battlefield. "A view of the entire line of battle from the extreme right to the extreme left, say from 6 to 8 miles was spread out

before me," he recalled. "The scene from this height & at this moment of the battle was magnificent beyond description. Language could not do it justice & any attempt to describe it would be useless & impotent in the extreme. It was a scene I never expect to live to see again. Surely no mortal ever witnessed one so fearfully sublime." The *Eagle* returned to earth after just 25 minutes, and high winds grounded it for the next two days. By the time it was again able to ascend, the battle was over.

Six weeks after the Battle of Fredericksburg, the Army of the Potomac gained a new commander, Gen. Joseph Hooker. "Fighting Joe" apparently agreed with the army wag who commented that "observation on the moon would disclose as much as to the movements of the enemy" as Professor Lowe's balloons "and would be of far more practical value...." Upon taking command Hooker cut Lowe's pay, reduced his staff, and did everything in his power to hinder his work. Lowe's patience snapped, and after the Battle of Chancellorsville he resigned his position in the army. With his departure, aerial observation in the Army of the Potomac came to an end.

An ascent in the *Intrepid*

Confederate guns in action on Telegraph Hill

Lee Directs the Battle from Telegraph Hill

"It is well that war is so terrible; or we would grow too fond of it." These words, among the most famous of the Civil War, were uttered by Gen. Robert E. Lee during the Battle of Fredericksburg from his command post atop Telegraph Hill. They express the divided emotions of a man who found attraction in the challenge, excitement and pageantry of war, while at the same time being repelled by its death and destruction.

Lee first made his headquarters at Telegraph Hill on Dec. 11. A message from officers near the town had notified the general that the Union army was crossing the Rappahannock River at Fredericksburg. Dressing hastily, he rode the five-mile distance from Hamilton's Crossing and established himself on the hill by early morning. Throughout the day he watched as a brigade of Mississippi riflemen kept the Union army at bay along the water's edge. In an effort to dislodge the Confederates, the Northern commander, Gen. Ambrose E. Burnside, ordered his artillery to shell the town. Five thousand or more shells crashed into the city, destroying walls and setting buildings ablaze. The sight made Lee's blood boil. "These people delight to destroy the weak and those who

can make no defense; it just suits them!" he fumed.

By evening, the Army of the Potomac had thrown pontoon bridges across the river at three places and appeared ready to occupy Fredericksburg in force. Lee's army held a strong position on the hills behind the town, but his outnumbered army was scattered over a 20-mile area. In an effort to concentrate his troops to meet an attack, Lee ordered "Stonewall" Jackson to bring up two of his four divisions from their positions south of town and place them on Prospect Hill, on the right end of his line. In the event that Burnside's efforts at Fredericksburg prove merely a ruse to cover a crossing farther downstream, Lee allowed Jackson's other two divisions to remain where they were.

Uncertainty as to Burnside's intentions vanished the following day. On Dec. 12 Lee accompanied Jackson out to the skirmish line and watched as tens of thousands of Union soldiers poured down Stafford Heights and across the pontoon bridges south of town. Certain now that the Union general intended to make his main attack at Fredericksburg, Lee ordered Jackson to bring up his remaining two divisions from their position near

Port Royal. When the Union army attacked, Lee would have his entire force on hand to meet it.

Dec. 13 dawned cool and foggy. Telegraph Hill was astir with artillerymen, staff officers and generals. Gen. James Longstreet joined Lee on the hill. Longstreet commanded half the troops in Lee's army, and at Fredericksburg he held the left and center of Lee's seven-mile line. Also present were Gens. Lafayette McLaws, commanding a division in Longstreet's corps, and William Nelson Pendleton, the army's chief of artillery. Jackson and cavalryman J.E.B. Stuart also appeared, having ridden up from Prospect Hill to receive their final instructions before the fighting began. Jackson chose the occasion to don a new uniform coat given to him as a gift by Stuart and a new hat encircled in gold braid recently sent to him by his wife. The sight of the normally plain-dressed general decked out in such finery caused tongues to wag. Some soldiers joked that Stonewall had drawn his bounty; others laughingly suggested that the general might be so worried about soiling his new clothes that he would not get down to work.

The banter continued after Jackson reached Lee's headquarters. By then the fog had lifted somewhat, giving the Confederate generals a peek at the enormous strength of the Union army. Northern might was particularly apparent on the plain below town, fronting Jackson's position. Longstreet, in an awkward attempt at humor, asked Jackson, "General, do not all these multitudes of Federals frighten you?" Jackson, a humorless man, replied simply: "We shall see very soon whether I shall not frighten them." Longstreet pursued the joke. "Jackson, what are you going to do with all those people over there?" With grow-

James Longstreet

ing fire in his voice, the earnest general replied, "Sir, we will give them the bayonet."

Burnside opened his attack against Jackson's corps. More than 50,000 Union soldiers — enough to fill a modern sports stadium — deployed in broad lines across the fields south of town, their flags snapping smartly in the winter breeze. It was this soul-stirring sight that undoubtedly prompted Lee's remark about the glory and horror of war. As the left wing of the Union army prepared to engage Jackson at Prospect Hill, the right wing advanced out of town and engaged Longstreet's men at Marye's Heights. By 1 p.m. the battle was raging furiously on both fronts. A momentary Union breakthrough on Jackson's part of the line gave Lee a few anxious moments, but it was the repeated Union attacks against Longstreet's position at Marye's Heights that worried him most.

"General, they are massing very heavily and will break your line, I am afraid," said Lee, turning to Longstreet.

"General, if you put every man now on the other side of the Potomac in that field to approach me over the same line, and give me plenty of ammunition, I will kill them all before they reach my line," replied Longstreet confidently. "Look to your right," he said nodding toward Jackson's position. "You are in some danger there, but not on my line."

Longstreet knew what he was talking about. Although more than 30,000 Union soldiers attacked Marye's Heights that afternoon, not a single man reached the Confederate line.

In addition to being Lee's headquarters, Telegraph Hill served as an important Confederate artillery position. More than a dozen cannon crowned the hill, including a huge rifled gun brought up from Richmond that was capable of hurling a 30-pound shell a distance of more than two miles. The Federals had large guns, too, however, and the cannon on Telegraph Hill soon drew fire from Union artillery on Stafford Heights. Lee narrowly escaped death when one Union shell struck an earthwork beside him but failed to explode.

The Confederates did not return the long-range fire of the Union batteries. Instead they saved their limited ammunition for Northern infantry on the plain below. As Union soldiers toiled toward Marye's Heights, Southern gunners on Telegraph Hill flayed the left flank of their lines with a savage fire. In an effort to escape the punishment, some Union soldiers sought shelter in the cut of an unfinished railroad that still exists just south of Lafayette Boulevard. But the safety of the ditch was an illusion. Confederate gunners on Telegraph Hill had a clear shot down the railroad. As Union soldiers packed into the cut, exploding shells sliced through the ranks, killing and maiming dozens. The railroad cut had become a death trap.

Things were only marginally safer on Telegraph Hill. While firing its 39th round, the large cannon from Richmond burst, sending the front half of the barrel whirling down the hillside, while the back half went flipping into the woods to the rear. Although Lee and Longstreet were standing nearby when the explosion occurred, miraculously

Lee and Longstreet on Telegraph Hill

neither they nor anyone else was injured in the mishap.

Today Telegraph Hill is Stop No. 2 on the Fredericksburg Battlefield tour. Now called Lee Hill, it is a place of quiet reflection. As one stands on its peaceful summit gazing out over the landscape that witnessed the struggle of a nation, Lee's paradoxical words come rushing back to the mind: "It is well that war is so terrible; or we would grow too fond of it."

Brompton

Fredericksburg boasts many historic homes, but few felt the heel of war more keenly than Brompton, a brick mansion that overlooks the intersection of Hanover Street and Sunken Road. Lawyer John L. Marye built Brompton sometime after 1821. Originally it was a rectangular structure, but Marye added wings and a porch to the building, giving it the graceful appearance that it still enjoys today. Marye had eight children, and laughter filled the hallways. Diarist Jane Beale attended a May Day celebration there in 1851. Seldom had she beheld a more lovely sight than the Marye girls and their friends preparing for the evening dance "dressed in white with blue sashes."

The Civil War brought an end to Brompton's gaiety. John Marye was a member of Virginia's secession convention. He hoped that the North and South would settle their differences amicably, but when peace negotiations failed Marye reluctantly joined a majority of other delegates in voting the state out of the Union. He little imagined the impact his decision would have on his family and his home.

For the first 18 months of the war, Fredericksburg suffered little from the war. Union troops occupied the town in the spring and summer of 1862, but there was no fighting, and the Union troops dealt gently with their hosts. That changed in November when opposing armies converged on the town for the Battle of Fredericksburg. Gen. Robert E. Lee, commanding the Confederate forces, occupied a seven-mile defensive line that stretched across the heights south and west of the town. Part of Lee's line ran along Marye's Heights, right past Brompton's front door. Marye saw the danger and wisely evacuated the house, moving to his in-laws' house, Forest Hill, south of town.

In the owner's absence, Col. James Walton made Brompton his headquarters. Walton commanded an artillery battalion in Lee's army, and nine of his guns crowned the heights. Below them, in a sunken section of the Telegraph Road, stood a brigade of Georgia riflemen led by Thomas R.R. Cobb. On Dec. 13, 1862, Union troops poured out of the town and attacked Marye's

Heights. Cobb's men easily repelled the assault, aided by Walton's guns on the ridge and by sharpshooters firing from the upper windows of the Marye House.

But the Union army was just beginning. Over the next eight hours no less than 18 brigades — more than 30,000 men — attacked Marye's Heights, prompting Lee to reinforce the position. At 2 p.m., he ordered four South Carolina regiments to join Cobb and Walton on the ridge. The 2nd and 8th South Carolina augmented Cobb's beleaguered men in the road; the 3rd and 7th South Carolina took position on the ridge above.

Col. James D. Nance commanded the 3rd South Carolina Regiment. Nance led his men past Brompton to an exposed knoll overlooking the road. Immediately he began to take heavy casualties. Nance ordered his men to lie down, but casualties continued to mount. The colonel was among the first hit. As he hurried to the right of his line, looking for a more sheltered position for his regiment, a bullet struck him in the thigh. Command passed to the unit's lieutenant colonel, but a Minié ball soon buried itself in his side. Other bullets incapacitated the regiment's major and senior captain. When the next ranking officer suffered a shattered leg, command of 3rd South Carolina passed to Capt. John C. Summer. Summer was not a religious man, and it was therefore with some surprise that a fellow officer found him on his knees in prayer before the battle. When the officer jokingly suggested that fear had prompted his friend's newfound piety, Summer replied seriously that he was going to die in the coming battle and thought it wise to make his peace with God.

His premonition proved accurate. Moments after taking command of the regiment, a bullet struck Summer in the head, killing him instantly. He was the sixth commander to fall. Reflecting on the regiment's exposed position in front of the house, a South Carolina soldier commented that it was "wonderful everyone was not either killed or wounded." As it was, 166 men were hit.

Brompton too suffered severely. A Confederate staff officer who visited the structure after the battle observed that "Not an inch of the surface of the bricks on the front of the house...was free from the mark of a Minié ball. Bushels of flattened ones were to be seen on the ground, while the woodwork was torn to pieces by them...." Another soldier wrote that the building had been "raked by musket balls until it looks as if a hail storm had scoured it."

A second round of Union assaults against Marye's Heights during the Chancellorsville Campaign in May 1863 only added to the damage. By

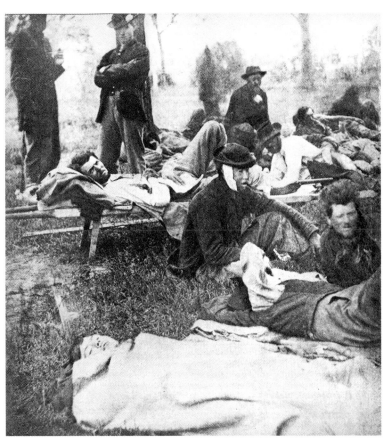

Union wounded at Brompton

battle's end Brompton was a battered shell of its former self. A man who visited the house in 1864 commented on the desolation. "Ah! it was a sad thing to thread the deserted halls and chambers of this old house and hear only the echo of your footsteps," he reflected. "Not even a rat squeaks behind the wainscot. The silence is awful." The damage extended beyond the house onto the grounds, which were scarred by earthworks and hasty graves.

Brompton's trials were not over. In May 1864, the Union and Confederate armies clashed again in the Wilderness and at Spotsylvania Court House. Overnight, Fredericksburg became a vast hospital, as ambulances and wagons rolled in from the west bearing more than 20,000 wounded soldiers. Ninth Corps surgeons commandeered Brompton, packing the house from cellar to garret with hundreds of injured men. Surgeon William Howell Reed described the suffering. "In one corner, upon a stretcher, lay a soldier.... He was wounded through the lungs, and breathed only with sharp stitches of pain. Another lad...was slowly wasting away. We kept him alive with stimulants and could not but feel that even this effort was a mockery." A third soldier lay "in the last agonies of death — a poor mutilated remnant of a man, and a most loathsome sight. His case was too bad to be placed with others, and he was laid carefully upon such ragged garments as we could collect for a bed, not enough to keep his shattered frame from the floor."

Conditions were horrid. "The poor fellows," Reed noted with pity, "had not had their clothes off since they were wounded, and were sleeping in blood and filth, and were swarming with vermin. They lay as close as they could be packed, the contaminated air growing worse every hour. The openings in the torn and battered walls assisted somewhat in ventilation." As the weather improved, many of the wounded were carried out of the stifling house and placed under a large oak tree on the east lawn. Nearby, soldiers dug a long trench in which to inter those who did not survive their wounds. After the war their remains would be moved down the ridge a few hundred yards and buried in Fredericksburg National Cemetery.

John Marye returned to Brompton in 1865 and began repairing the house. After his death in 1868, his heirs sold the estate to John G. Lane. Lane's family then sold the property to Capt. Maurice B. Rowe, who turned it into a thriving dairy farm. As years passed, many Union and Confederate veterans stopped to see the house that had played such a large part in their lives. One veteran even asked to be married there. As he explained to the owner, "he was unable to take Marye's Heights by storm in December of '62, [and] that he wanted to take it now in his own way by being married there."

Today the house is the private residence of Mary Washington College's president. Although Brompton is not open to the public, you can get a good view of it from the Sunken Road and from Hanover Street. If you look hard, you may be able to see a Civil War trench that slants across the front yard. What you won't be able to see are the hundreds of bullet marks that still scar the brick walls — vivid reminders of the violence that once engulfed the house.

Brompton as a dairy farm

Stephens House

Martha Stephens: Heroine or Hoax?

Among the most enduring, if least substanti-ated, legends surrounding the Battle of Fredericksburg is that of Martha Stephens, a woman who stubbornly refused to leave her home so that she could aid and comfort wounded sol-diers. But is the story true? You decide.

Martha Stephens (or Stevens) is an elusive — not to say shadowy — figure. She appears to have been born west of Fredericksburg, possibly in Culpeper County, around 1824. Her maiden name was Farrow. When still a teenager, she took a man named Elijah Innis (or Ennis) as her com-mon-law husband and had two children by him. By 1850 she was living outside of Fredericksburg on what is now Sunken Road. Innis had disap-peared by then, and by 1860 Martha was living with a 36-year-old local cabinetmaker named Ed-ward N. Stephens. The unmarried couple had two children, Mary and Agnes.

Martha lived a hard life, particularly after the disappearance of her first husband. The 1850 cen-sus shows her occupying a small house with eight others: her two oldest children, a sister, a mother (or mother-in-law), a 57-year-old man (possibly her mother's consort), and three young women who do not appear to have been related to the family.

The census taker listed 25-year-old Martha as the head of this heterogeneous clan. She sup-ported them by running a small grocery and speakeasy out of her house. That was hardly enough to feed so many mouths, however, and the presence of the three young women under her roof, taken with other evidence, suggests that Martha may have operated a house of prostitution. Whatever her business, she did reasonably well for herself. During her lifetime she would purchase seven plots of land in Fredericksburg plus a 92-acre farm in Spotsylvania County.

Martha's activities made her a pariah in

Fredericksburg. A Confederate officer who visited the town after the Civil War described her as "a woman of abandoned character and an outcast of society." In addition to running a bar and perhaps a brothel, she was outspoken, not at all religious, and had a coarse manner about her. Moreover, she smoked a pipe and there are indications that later in her life she took up residence with a former slave. Although much of this is hearsay and cannot be proven, it is clear that Martha Stephens delighted in violating the social customs of her day.

Stephens would be forgotten was it not for the Civil War. In December 1862, Union and Confederate forces clashed at Fredericksburg in what was the largest battle up to that time in America. The Southern battle line ran down the Sunken Road, directly past Martha's front door. Gen. Thomas R.R. Cobb of Georgia commanded the troops in the road and established his headquarters in the Stephens house. Alarmed by the prospect of battle, Martha sent her children to safety, but chose herself to remain at the house.

The Union army focused its Dec. 13, 1862, attacks on Marye's Heights. For eight hours the Stephens house, at the base of the ridge, was at the center of a leaden storm. Hundreds of bullets crashed through the small wooden structure, and nearly 10,000 men were killed or wounded within sight of her porch. Among the casualties was Gen. Cobb, who was struck by a Union artillery shell just outside the house. He died a few hours later.

Where was Martha at this trying time? According to local sources, she was at her home binding the wounds of Union and Confederate soldiers. Maj. W. Roy Mason, who lived at "The Sentry Box" on Caroline Street, wrote that Martha "attended the wounded and the dying fearless of consequences.... It is said that after using all the materials for bandages at her command, she tore from her person most of her garments, even on that bitter cold day, in her anxiety to administer to the necessities greater than her own." Later historians embroidered the theme. In 1912, Judge John Goolrick wrote that Martha did what she could, "bandaging hurts until the bandages gave out. She tore into strips what cloth there was

in the little meager house — her sheets, her towels, her tablecloths, her poor wardrobe. When all was gone, she tore her calico dress.... She was a veritable heroine in that great drama of war," he concluded.

Historian Alvin Embrey, writing eight years after Goolrick, insisted that Martha not only bound the wounds of injured soldiers but brought them water from her well. She went about her merciful tasks unmindful of the bullets and shells that filled the air, "as if she alone...were immune to death...." Embrey too repeats the story of Martha tearing up her dress after she had exhausted her supply of other bandages, adding that after the battle the intrepid lady was ashamed "to find herself in the presence of Gen. Lee with her dress cut off from her knees to the ground." A modest woman!

Martha Stephens' legend gained national currency in 1935 when Douglas Southall Freeman included it in his Pulitzer-Prize-winning biography of Robert E. Lee. In his book Freeman, citing Embrey, quoted the general as saying at the height of the battle, "I wish those people would let Mrs. Stevens alone!" In his later work, *Lee's Lieutenants,* Freeman repeated the tale adding, on the basis of Goolrick's and Embrey's accounts, that Gen. Cobb was treated at the Stephens house and expired there.

Unfortunately, none of this has any solid basis in fact. None of the three early writers, Mason, Embrey and Goolrick, witnessed Martha Stephens' heroics; indeed Embrey had not been born yet. Each of the writers had gotten his information from Martha Stephens herself years after the war ended. Of the thousands of soldiers who were present in the Sunken Road on Dec. 13, not one mentions Martha Stephens being there, much less performing deeds of courage and compassion. That such heroism by a civilian could have gone unnoticed is unthinkable. Confederate newspapers would have vied with one another in trumpeting Martha Stephens' fortitude and valor. Yet not one soldier — not even Gen. Joseph Kershaw, who occupied the Stephens house as his headquarters during the

battle — so much as mentioned her name.

One aspect of the legend is clearly false. Contemporary sources make it clear that Gen. Cobb was not taken into the Stephens house after his wounding, as later writers suggested, and Martha Stephens certainly did not treat him. Instead, aides carried Cobb down the Telegraph Road to a field hospital located at the Wiet house, near the site of the modern Spotswood Baptist Church. He expired there a short time later.

Why would Martha Stephens fabricate such a story? Two motives come to mind. The first is money. Martha had an entrepreneurial spirit, and she realized that her riddled house might one day be a tourist attraction. She adamantly refused to have it repaired. "Thousands visit it annually," reported veteran J.O. Kerbey, "and perhaps, she reaps a richer harvest from the tourists who usually contribute something by way of compensation for the damage, and for her trouble in explaining it all." In at least one instance, Martha sold a bullet-ridden clapboard to a tourist for a dollar. For her, the Civil War had become a cash cow.

A second motive Martha may have had for inventing the story was respect. As noted earlier, she had been a social outcast in Fredericksburg prior to the Civil War. What better way to redeem her reputation than to transform herself into a model of bravery and compassion? Initially most townspeople didn't buy it, but as the years wore on and those who knew the truth died out, Martha's story took hold. In fact, it more than took hold — it took off. With the publication of the story by Freeman, she became not only a local legend, but a national legend as well.

By then, Martha Stephens was long dead. She had died at her home in 1888, a quarter century following the battle that had scarred her house and redeemed her reputation. The house itself succumbed to fire in 1913. Today a small monument marks the site of her deeds — real or fictitious — and Martha herself lies buried in a small cemetery plot nearby. Although she is gone, she is certainly not forgotten.

Ambrose Burnside Goes for Broke

It was the afternoon of Dec. 13, 1862, and things were going badly for the Union army — very badly. Gen. Ambrose E. Burnside had ordered two assaults against the Confederate line at Fredericksburg. The first and largest assault was made by Gen. William B. Franklin against "Stonewall" Jackson's part of the line, south of town. The second assault was made by Gen. Edwin V. Sumner against James Longstreet's Confederates at Marye's Heights. But as they often do in war, things had gone terribly wrong. Franklin had gotten a late start, and when he finally did attack he committed only a fraction of his force. Jackson defeated him soundly. On Sumner's front, Union troops swept across an open plain toward Marye's Heights only to be cut down by Confederates ensconced behind a stout stone wall. Sumner repeatedly attacked the Confederates, but nothing could budge them. In short, the Union army was in a fix, and its befuddled commander did not know what to do. Should he cancel the ill-advised attacks and look for an opportunity to retreat or should he throw in the rest of his army in one last desperate stab at victory? Burnside decided to go for broke.

Gen. Joseph "Fighting Joe" Hooker commanded the last of Burnside's three grand divisions. At 2:30 Burnside ordered Gen. Franklin to renew his assault against Jackson's line. At the same time he directed Hooker to cross the Rappahannock River and support Sumner's attacks against the stone wall. Hooker's grand division consisted of the Third and Fifth corps. Because he had sent the Third Corps to reinforce Franklin earlier that day, he had just one corps — the Fifth — available to use against Marye's Heights.

Hooker opposed the attack. After viewing the strength of the Confederate position, he concluded that additional assaults there would be simply a waste of life. He sent word back to Burnside urging him to cancel the attack, then rode to army headquarters to plead his case. But Burnside would not listen. He ordered Hooker to advance at once.

Discouraged, "Fighting Joe" rode back into town to prepare for the assault. The only chance he had of capturing the heights, he decided, was if he first battered the Confederates into submission with artillery fire. He accordingly ordered every available battery to open on the heights. When their distant fire seemed to have no effect, Gen. Darius Couch settled on a desperate measure. He ordered his chief of artillery, Col. Charles Morgan, to push a

Joseph Hooker

battery all the way to the front and blast the Confederates at close range. Morgan did not like the idea. At that distance, his gunners would be easy targets for the Southern riflemen behind the wall. "General, a battery can't live there," Morgan protested. "Then it must die there!" Couch replied. Morgan insisted that Couch would lose his guns. "I would rather lose my guns than lose my men," the general snapped. "Put them in."

Morgan selected Capt. John G. Hazard's Rhode Island battery for the task. Around 4 p.m. Hazard's six guns clattered across a makeshift bridge constructed over a canal ditch located at the intersection of present-day Hanover Street and Kenmore Avenue. They unlimbered on the rise beyond, less than 200 yards from the stone wall. For half an hour Hazard's pieces banged away, doing minimal damage to the Confederates behind the wall. In that time, the battery lost 16 men and 12 horses. Considering its proximity to the Confederate line, the battery's losses had been surprisingly light. "I supposed that Hazard would be entirely annihilated," Couch later admitted.

Hooker's men meanwhile joined Sumner's troops on the firing line. Charles Griffin's division went in on the left, advancing from the railroad depot toward Marye's Heights along the path of modern Lafayette Boulevard. On the way the men passed a brickyard, where wounded soldiers had

crawled to find protection. Instead, it turned out to be a death trap. Confederate shells smashed into the bricks, shattering them into deadly fragments. A Pennsylvanian in Griffin's division noted that the "mangled, bleeding forms" of the wounded men "lay strewn everywhere, closely packed together."

Griffin's men swept past the brickyard and toward the heights under a galling fire. "It seemed to me that men were falling all around me," remembered one terrified soldier. "Bullets spoke to me zip! whiz! bang!! and the shells screeched! Horrible! It was so new to me and wild; and the men hurrying to shelter or rear, with blood streaming from their wounds, or moaning. To say this is awful is tame; it cannot be described. If this is war," he concluded, "I want to see no more of it."

The division continued toward the heights, its ranks thinning with each step. One man remembered that the soldiers instinctively leaned forward "as though they were breasting a storm of rain and sleet, their faces and bodies being only half turned to the storm, with their shoulders shrugged." As they neared the wall, Griffin's lead brigade encountered a 5-foot-high board fence. Some soldiers clambered over the obstruction; others paused to batter it down. Beyond it, face down on the ground, lay the shattered, bleeding remnants of Sumner's grand division. Griffin's men threw themselves into mud beside Sumner's men and joined them in firing at the almost invisible line of Confederates behind the stone wall. Bullets struck the ground all around them. In an effort to escape harm, some Union soldiers pushed dirt up in front of them; others used their blanket rolls for protection. A few even fashioned breastworks from the bodies of deceased comrades. It was a horrid scene, remembered a Confederate artilleryman, "the very saturnalia of death."

Meanwhile, several hundred yards to the north, Gen. Andrew A. Humphreys' division was wading into action. Most of Humphreys' men never had been in battle before, and as the shells screamed over their heads many soldiers involuntarily ducked or "juked," to use a phrase common at the time. Dodging enemy shells was unbecoming in a soldier and did no good, and Humphreys determined to put a stop to it. Over the roar of battle the grizzled veteran shouted out, "Don't juke, boys!" Just then a particularly large shell whizzed past Humphreys' head, causing him to duck. Despite the danger, the soldiers had a hearty laugh at their commander's expense. Humphreys was embarrassed, but he rose to the occasion. In a moment of inspiration, he shouted: "Juke the big ones, boys, but don't mind the little ones!"

The general had two brigades, one led by Col. Peter H. Allabach, the other by Gen. Erastus B. Tyler. There was room at the front for only one brigade at a time. Leaving Tyler back near the millrace (modern Kenmore Avenue), Humphreys led Allabach's men toward the wall. When they reached the front, they came under a torrent of fire. Instead of continuing forward, Allabach's men instinctively took cover in a shallow ravine 150 yards from the wall. In doing so, they joined thousands of other Union soldiers who were already there. With great effort, Humphreys got Allabach's men back on their feet and moving again, but the attack's momentum was gone. The brigade got within 30 yards of the wall before recoiling under the blasts of the Confederate rifles. Staggering toward the rear, Allabach's men rejoined their comrades in the muddy defile.

With the sun now setting, Humphreys brought up his last brigade. Having seen the futility of exchanging fire with the Confederates, Humphreys ordered Tyler's men to fix bayonets. They would take the stone wall with cold steel. With a cheer Tyler's men started at a double quick across the plain. Bullets shredded their ranks with each step. Humphreys had two horses shot from under him. As Tyler's men approached the ravine, Union soldiers there waved at them to go back. No one could pass that point and live! Some soldiers went so far as to grab the legs of Tyler's men as they passed, pulling them to the ground. The effect was disastrous. The brigade became disordered and slowed to a halt. Although Humphreys got it going again, its momentum was gone. Like Allabach's brigade a few minutes before, Tyler's brigade dissolved into the growing darkness. With Humphreys' repulse, the Union defeat was complete. "Finding that I had lost as many men as my order required me to lose," Hooker testified bitterly, "I suspended the attack...."

Gen. Burnside had risked everything and had lost. His army, defeated and demoralized, now stood with its back to the river, inviting attack. Burnside never had wanted command of the army; he had insisted that he was not qualified to lead it, but President Lincoln and his advisers had not believed him. Perhaps they would believe him now.

Hazard's Battery goes into action

The Battle of Fredericksburg

Loading Union wounded aboard ship bound for Washington hospitals

One Man's Ordeal: The Story of William McCarter

The Battle of Fredericksburg was the most costly battle the North had suffered up to that point in the Civil War. According to official returns, the Army of the Potomac suffered 12,653 casualties in fight. Of that number, exactly 9,600 were wounded. Many of those men would die later as a result of their wounds; others would suffer painful, often crippling, effects for the rest of their lives. This story is about one man's tribulations as a wounded soldier at Fredericksburg, but it accurately reflects the experience of thousands.

The subject of our story is William McCarter, a 21-year-old Irish immigrant with a wife and children. At the time of the war, he was employed as a leatherworker in Philadelphia. Responding to his adopted country's call, McCarter enlisted as a private in the 116th Pennsylvania Volunteers, a regiment in the Irish Brigade. The brigade's commander, Gen. Thomas F. Meagher, needed a clerk at his headquarters, and when he saw an example of McCarter's impeccable handwriting, he gave him the job.

The Army of the Potomac occupied Fredericksburg in December 1862 and prepared to attack the Confederate army, which was drawn up on the heights outside of town. Gen. Meagher told McCarter to remain at his headquarters in Stafford County, but like most young men who never had been in a battle McCarter was eager to taste combat. Ignoring the general's orders, he crossed the Rappahannock River and joined the 116th Pennsylvania in its attack on Marye's Heights. What he experienced there erased any notions that he may have had about the glory of war. As the Irish Brigade charged across the plain leading to the ridge, Confederate cannon and rifle fire decimated the Union ranks. In the 116th Pennsylvania the losses were staggering. "Every third man had fallen," wrote McCarter, "and along some parts of the line, every second soldier had been killed or wounded. To make matters still worse, we had lost nearly all our Officers."

Bullets filled the air. One spent ball struck McCarter on the left shoulder, giving him a large bruise; another clipped his ankle inflicting a painful, if not dangerous, wound. A Minié ball pierced the cartridge box at his side, while others cut through his uniform. McCarter continued to fight on despite wounds to himself and those around him. A young man standing next to him was shot in the stomach. "He rolled about for a few minutes in agony and blood, two or three yards in front of me," remembered McCarter, "and with the exclamation: 'Oh, my mother!' on his lips, he died." Moments later a soldier standing immediately behind him went down. Then it was McCarter's turn. As he was ramming a new round down the barrel of his rifle, a ball struck the young clerk in the arm, just below the right shoulder. "A stream of warm blood rushed out of the wound, saturating my clothing down to my feet, the shattered arm dropped powerless by my side; dizziness and partial loss of sight followed, and I fell unconscious on the ground."

When McCarter came to, he found the tempest at its height. "...Bullets kept constantly whizzing over me, around me, burying themselves in the ground not a foot from my head and throwing mud and dust all over my person. My situation was truly an awful one." The body of a dead comrade lay between McCarter and the Confederate line. Lying down behind it, McCarter used the corpse as a makeshift barricade. By the end of the afternoon it was riddled with bullets.

As night fell, the Union army withdrew to the city, leaving a strong skirmish line in front of the heights. McCarter and many other injured soldiers lay between the lines, subject not only to Confederate fire, but to the errant fire of their own men. "I now gave myself up for lost," he admitted, "never expecting to leave or to be removed from that spot alive."

McCarter gathered his dwindling strength, however, and as darkness covered the field, he slowly dragged himself to the rear. Every 10 minutes or so the Confederates fired a volley to discourage a surprise attack. The flash of the rifles briefly illuminated the Southern riflemen who, to McCarter, understandably looked "more like devils than human beings." Moving little by little between volleys, he eventually reached the millrace now covered by modern Kenmore Avenue. Because of the large number of corpses there,

McCarter called the place "The Valley of Death." By then he was dehydrated from loss of blood and his strength was spent. "I felt as though I was being consumed, the pains of my wounds increased, and my...tongue literally stuck fast to the roof of my mouth, almost preventing articulation. My sufferings now from the pains of my wounds were indeed light compared with my suffering from 'thirst,' and I really prayed to God, with all my soul, to end my life then, and there, or send me water."

After an hour, a dim blue flame flickered in the distance — two soldiers looking for wounded comrades. McCarter tried to call for help, but he was too weak to move and his mouth was too dry to speak. He could hope only that they saw him. God was with McCarter that night, for the men saw him, and they also happened to belong to his own company. Greedily, he drank the water that ran from their canteens — a full quart, he later estimated. The men did not have a stretcher, and McCarter was too feeble to walk. Fortunately an ambulance appeared, but it was already carrying 11 others. McCarter's friends persuaded the driver to take one more, and the overloaded vehicle soon was making its way into town. To the agony of the wounded soldiers inside, it seemed to hit every rock, stump and rut along the way. The passengers pleaded with the driver to go more slowly, but he ignored their cries. Two men died before they reached the town.

The ambulance finally halted in front of a four-story house that, like nearly all the buildings in town, was being used as a hospital. Revived by the water he had received, McCarter limped into the building under his own power and lay down in an elegant room alongside seven other wounded soldiers. During the night additional ambulances discharged their human cargo. By morning dozens of men filled the room. The first surgeons did not make their appearance until after sunrise. They slowly moved about, examining each man. When they got to McCarter, they cut the blood-soaked clothing away from his body and probed his injured arm for the bullet. They found it, and with-

Wounded soldiers in Fredericksburg, May 1864

out using any anesthesia, cut the leaden ball from the soldier's body, giving it to him as a "relic of the war."

McCarter remained in the makeshift hospital for just one day. The Union army was retreating, and as the first step in that operation, it sent its wounded soldiers across the river to Stafford County. Unlike many others, McCarter was able to walk. He joined thousands of other injured soldiers who slowly made their way across the pontoon bridge to Falmouth Station, a train depot located just behind modern Earl's Shopping Center. For hours he stood in the cold mud before fi-

nally boarding a train that took him to Aquia Landing on the Potomac River (now Aquia Landing Park). There, after another considerable wait, he found passage aboard a special steamboat that carried him to a hospital in Washington.

McCarter's injury prevented him from returning to the army. His arm suffered permanent damage, and after spending five months in a hospital ward he was discharged from the service. Ironically, he returned to Fredericksburg in 1885 and resided there for one year. He died in Washington in 1911 at the age of 71.

Chatham, 1863

Chatham Feels the Hand of War

During the Battle of Fredericksburg, the City of Fredericksburg became one vast hospital. Nearly 10,000 Union soldiers — a number twice the size of the town's population in 1860 — came streaming back from the front with ghastly wounds to the head, arms, legs and body. To accommodate these injured men, nearly every building in the area became a field hospital. Among the largest of these was Chatham.

Chatham is a magnificent old house overlooking the Rappahannock River. In 1862 it was the home of the Lacy family — or at least it had been until the spring of that year, when Union troops occupied the dwelling. Betty's husband, James Horace, was serving as a major in the Confederate army, and Betty did not feel safe remaining in the house by herself. She and her children moved across the river to stay with friends in town, later joining Maj. Lacy in the southwestern part of the state.

Gen. Irvin McDowell meanwhile occupied Chatham and used it as his headquarters. McDowell had commanded the Union forces at Bull Run, the first battle of the Civil War. Now, nine months later, he was in charge of the Department of the Rappahannock, a geographical area covering all of northern Virginia. Mrs. Lacy would

have been shocked to learn that McDowell hosted President Lincoln at her house, but otherwise he was an ideal tenant, inflicting minimal damage on the house during his brief stay.

The same could not be said for the grounds. Prior to the war, Chatham boasted beautiful shade trees, a terraced yard, and a fabulous garden. McDowell's occupation destroyed much of that. A Union soldier noted that the manicured grounds that had surrounded the house "were now covered with the tents of staff officers and orderlies; the fences were gone, the shrubbery destroyed, and the whole plain, now covered with troops, was, aside from the bustle of marshaling hosts, a barren, uninviting waste."

It was but a sample of what lay ahead. The Union army returned to the area late in the year to fight the Battle of Fredericksburg. Again Chatham became a headquarters for Union officers. Gen. Orlando Willcox used the building for several days in November 1862, and Willcox's boss, Gen. Edwin Sumner, made it his command post on Dec. 13, the day of the heaviest fighting. To soldiers used to sleeping in tents, Chatham was a welcome change. In a letter to his wife, Willcox described sitting in "a quaint old-fashioned room with green high wainscoting" at the end of the house. "At night, by the fire in the grate, in the perfect stillness & with the old time furniture, I can scarcely help falling into fantastic reveries," he mused. "It is such a room as would please an author...."

The rooms so admired by Willcox soon would be ravaged by war. The fighting at Fredericksburg resulted in 9,600 Union soldiers being wounded, many of whom were treated at the house. Capt. Wesley Brainerd of the 50th New York Engineers was among the first Union soldiers to arrive. Brainerd was in charge of building one of six pontoon bridges that the Union army used to cross the river. On Dec. 11, while construction of the bridges was in progress, Confederate sharpshooters fired at the engineers. A bullet struck Brainerd in the arm. He was carried into Chatham feeling, he wrote, like "a lifeless lump of lead." Brainerd's attendants placed him in a chair, but the weakened officer soon slumped unconscious to the ground. When he awoke, he found the room "filled with the wounded, dead and dying. Some were crying, some groaning and others were too far gone to do either." A surgeon bound Brainerd's wound and later sent him from "that horrid place" to a hospital farther to the rear.

Others took his place. Sgt. Josiah F. Murphey of the 20th Massachusetts was shot in the face that afternoon and, like Brainerd, was brought back to Chatham. Murphey's attendants laid him in the corner of a room next to a wounded Confederate from Mississippi. An hour later, they brought a man from Murphey's regiment into the room. The soldier had a nasty wound and was crying out in pain. "As soon as he caught sight of me," wrote Murphey, "he begged me piteously to kill him and end his suffering." The man received a painkiller instead.

Not all were fortunate enough to find lodging inside Chatham. As casualties mounted, the house filled up, forcing orderlies to place patients outside on the cold, damp ground. Murphey reflected on their suffering. "Think of it, wounded and unable to help yourself, and lying on the ground in the month of December with only a rubber blanket between you and the cold earth; but it could not be helped." Some of the unfortunate men later gained admittance to the house, he noted, by taking the place of those who died.

Volunteers assisted Union surgeons in caring for the wounded. Clara Barton arrived at Chatham on Dec. 8, three days before the battle. A private citizen, Barton had come to Fredericksburg specifically to aid the wounded should there be a battle. From her room on the second floor of the house, she could see the rows of Union tents stretched endlessly before her. Inside were soldiers, many of whom, she knew, would not survive the coming conflict. "...As I gazed sorrowfully upon them I thought I could almost hear the slow flap of the grim messenger's wings," she wrote, "as one by one he sought and selected his victims for the morning sacrifice." Wounded soldiers began streaming in on Dec. 11. Forty-eight hours later the stream had become a flood. They "covered every foot of the floors and porticos," Barton reported. They lay on stair landings, under tables, even in cupboards! Blood ran freely across the wooden floors, saturating the bottom of her dress, but she simply wrung it out and kept on working. There was no time to rest.

Poet Walt Whitman came to Chatham on Dec. 21 in search of a brother who had been wounded in the fighting. The battle was then

Clara Barton

Chatham

a week old, but the situation had not improved materially. "The house is quite crowded," he noted critically, "everything impromptu, no system, all bad enough, but I have no doubt the best that can be done; all the wounds pretty bad, some frightful, the men in their old clothes, unclean and bloody." Whitman picked his way through the building, stopping now and then to write letters for wounded men or to talk to those "who seemed most susceptible to it." Among those he met was a 19-year-old Mississippi captain — the same man Josiah Murphey had seen 10 days earlier. The young man had lost a leg and his face was pale, but his eyes still shone "bright as a hawk." Whitman would run into him again three months later at a hospital in Washington.

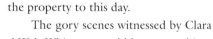

Walt Whitman

Walking outside the house, the poet stumbled upon a gruesome sight: "a heap of feet, legs, arms, and human fragments, cut, bloody, black and blue, swelled and sickening" — about enough, he estimated, to fill "a one-horse cart." The dismem-bered body parts had been tossed out a window by surgeons working inside the house and had piled up at the foot of a tree — possibly one of the gnarled catalpas that still graces *Chatham*'s front lawn. A few yards away, an even more horrid sight met his gaze — a line of corpses, covered with brown woolen blankets, awaiting burial. In all, more than 130 Union soldiers were buried at *Chatham*, their rude graves marked by a barrel stave or piece of broken board. Most were removed later to Fredericksburg National Cemetery, but three graves remain on the property to this day.

The gory scenes witnessed by Clara Barton and Walt Whitman would be repeated in May 1863, during the Chancellorsville Campaign, when Chatham again became a field hospital. The Lacys returned to the house in 1865, and the building remained a private residence until 1975. Today it is the headquarters of Fredericksburg and Spotsylvania County Battlefields Memorial National Military Park.

The Battle of Fredericksburg

Union artillery on Stafford Heights, 1863

Lee Misses His Chance

It was the night of Dec. 13, 1862. The Battle of Fredericksburg was over. The Union army had lost. Like a wounded animal, it lay bloodied and battered with its back to the Rappahannock River awaiting attack by Robert E. Lee's victorious Confederates. In front of Marye's Heights, within easy rifle range of Confederate soldiers in the sunken road, a line of Union soldiers tenaciously held the ground they had won during the day. Among them was Lt. Col. Joshua Chamberlain of the 20th Maine Volunteers. As Chamberlain lay in the cold mud, a plaintive wail drifted over the battlefield, like the moan of the winter wind: the sound of wounded soldiers dying helplessly nearby. The sound had no distinct source. Rather it seemed to Chamberlain that a thousand discordant voices had blended together "into a key-note — weird, unearthly, terrible to hear and bear." What made it all the more terrible was that neither he nor anyone else could help the sufferers. They lay in the no-man's land that separated the Union and Confederate lines. Any attempt to succor them meant almost certain death.

In an effort to shield himself from the chilling wind, Chamberlain lay down between two other soldiers. Whether they were asleep or dead he could not tell, nor did he care. The carnage of that frightful day had made the former Bowdoin College professor callous to such distinctions. "...The living and the dead were alike to me," he remembered. A third body lay at Chamberlain's head. Pulling the skirt of the man's coat over his face, Chamberlain tried to get some sleep. He had just drifted off when a hand pulled the garment away and a "half vampire-like" visage stared intently into his face. It was a soldier looking the body of a friend. The man started when Chamberlain spoke, not expecting to find the living among the dead. He moved on, and Chamberlain resumed his uneasy sleep. Nearby a window blind flapped mournfully in the wind, as if to say, "Never — forever; Forever — never!"

Chamberlain was not alone in his macabre vigil. A few hundred yards away a soldier in the 1st Minnesota Volunteers likewise sought shelter from the bone-chilling winds by crawling under the blanket of a comrade. When he awoke, he found he had been resting next to a corpse. "With cold chills creeping all over me I sought my place in the ranks and tried to 'forget it,'" he recalled. He never would.

The Union army's commander was also awake that night. Gen. Ambrose E. Burnside clattered across a pontoon bridge into town after midnight, Dec. 14, to confer with his officers in Fredericksburg. The commander "was cheerful in his tone and did not seem greatly oppressed," remembered Gen. Darius Couch, "but it was plain that he felt he had led us to a great disaster, and one knowing him so long and well as myself could see that he wished his body was also lying in front of Marye's Heights. I never felt so badly for a man in my life."

Gen. William F. "Baldy" Smith also witnessed the general's despair. Walking into his commanding general's tent the following day, Smith found Burnside walking up and down, alone and distracted, "apparently in great distress of mind." Seeing Smith, Burnside blurted out, "Oh! those men! oh! those men!" When Smith asked him what he meant, Burnside pointed across the river toward Marye's Heights, where thousands of his men lay dead or dying on the frosty turf. "I am thinking of them all the time," he said.

As dawn approached, Burnside issued orders to the army for another attack on Marye's Heights. This time, instead of attacking in waves, as he had done before, he would mass the Ninth Corps — his old command — in the Hazel Run Valley and rush the Heights in a column of regiments: a solid block of men some 36 files deep and perhaps 200 ranks wide. The general's orders left his subordinates aghast. Such a compact formation would make a perfect target for the Confederate cannons crowning the ridge. More astonishing still, Burnside proposed to lead the charge himself. Mounted on a horse in full view of enemy riflemen, he would certainly be among the first to fall. Perhaps that is what Burnside had in mind. Having ordered thousands of other men to their deaths the previous day, he may now have wished to sacrifice his own life as well.

Fortunately, reason prevailed. The morning

Joshua Chamberlain

that the attack was to occur, Gen. Edwin Sumner came to Burnside and urged him to reconsider the assault. "General, I hope you will desist from this attack; I do not know of any general officer who approves of it, and I think it will prove disastrous to the army." Such advice from the army's most aggressive officer gave Burnside pause. At Sumner's suggestion, he called a council of war to solicit the opinions of the army's other top officers. Without dissent, they agreed that another attack against Marye's Heights would be nothing short of slaughter. Burnside reluctantly bowed to the majority will. Canceling the attack, he made arrangements to bring his army back across the Rappahannock River.

As word of Burnside's decision filtered down through the ranks, the men of the Ninth Corps heaved a collective sigh of relief. "He has a great deal of confidence in his old corpse," wrote Pvt. James Gormley in a telling but unintentional slip of the pen, "but I am afraid it would have been the last of it if they had went up there." The Ninth Corps would have taken the battery-studded hill had it been ordered to do so, William Taylor of the 100th Pennsylvania Volunteers thought, "but it would have cost three fourths of their number to do it, and the other fourth would be 'blown to Kingdom Come' in five minutes after they took it." The surgeon of the 11th Connecticut Volunteers agreed. "It was virtually devoting the regiment to a glorious death," he concluded.

Meanwhile Robert E. Lee patiently waited for Burnside to renew the attack. He felt that his opponent could not abandon the offensive without at least one more effort: the people in the North would not allow it. As if to confirm that view, Confederate pickets early on Dec. 14 captured a

Union courier who carried a copy of Burnside's order to attack Marye's Heights. Armed with this inside information, Lee strengthened his position and confidently awaited Burnside's assault. But to Lee's puzzlement, the day passed in relative quiet. Had the Union general changed his mind, or was he simply awaiting the arrival of reinforcements from northern Virginia?

Union soldiers were puzzled, too — not by Burnside's inactivity, but rather by Lee's. The Confederate general had them trapped with their backs against the Rappahannock. Why didn't he attack and finish them off? The answer stood on the bluffs behind them. The Union commander had more than 100 guns deployed across Stafford Heights. Had the Confederates tried to attack the Union army near the river, Burnside's cannon would have torn them to pieces.

But why did Lee not shell the town? Half the Union army was packed into Fredericksburg's narrow streets. Southern artillerymen could have killed or maimed thousands without any danger to themselves by simply shelling the town. "Why they did not fire on us while were in the city I cannot imagine," wrote one perplexed, yet re- lieved, Union soldier. "...Had they opened on us while laying there...they would have slaughtered the whole corps, and we were expecting it too." Some historians have suggested that Lee refrained from shelling Fredericksburg out of consideration for civilians still trapped in the town. Others ar- gued that he did not want to inflict further dam- age on Fredericksburg's houses and businesses. Neither explanation seems valid. After all, Lee's guns had shelled the town intermittently nearly every day since the Union army had crossed. More likely, he withheld his blow in the hope that Burnside would renew his disastrous attacks. Once he had given the Union army a second drubbing, Lee would go over to the offensive.

Lack of ammunition too may have factored into his decision. After the battle Confederate gunners admitted to Union soldiers that they were low on shot and shell. They had ordered addi- tional ammunition from Richmond, but the new supply had arrived one day too late. Whatever the reason for Lee's inaction, he missed a golden op portunity to inflict added damage on the enemy. He would not get a second chance.

Flag of truce to bury the dead

Two Days of Suspense

For the Army of the Potomac, the days following the Battle of Fredericksburg were ones of fear and confusion. The Union army had been whipped, and it now stood with its back to the Rappahannock River awaiting — one might add, dreading — a Confederate attack that might complete its annihilation.

The attacks of Dec. 13, 1862, had thinned the army's ranks and shattered its organization. Men wandered about the town searching for their regiments — or what was left of them. The 24th New Jersey Volunteers mustered just 36 men the day after the battle; the Irish Brigade was able to rally less than one-quarter of the 1,200 it had taken into the fight. Had the Confederates assaulted the town that morning, they might have destroyed a large portion of the Union army, but Lee held his men in check, hoping perhaps that his counterpart, Gen. Ambrose E. Burnside, would be foolish enough to attack him again.

Northern soldiers replenished their ammunition and cleaned their rifles in anticipation of renewed hostilities then wandered off in search of food and plunder. But the ravaged town had little left to give. Every building had been ransacked; every store and business, looted. Some soldiers managed to crack safes at the local banks, but they profited little from their effort.

In one instance the earth yielded that which the buildings could not give. A soldier in a Rhode Island battery camped near Federal Hill, a house near the intersection of Hanover and Prince Edward streets, noticed a wooden headboard in the yard on which a civilian had carved the words "Our Little Willie." Suspicious, the soldier got a shovel and started to dig. A few feet down he struck a box, which, when opened, revealed eight smoked hams. "...We were all of us cannibals," he crowed, "eating 'Little Willie' for a week after...."

Sgt. Thomas Bowen of the 12th United

States Infantry was on picket duty throughout Dec. 14. Relieved at midnight, he walked back into town on streets littered with debris. On the way he passed men eating from fine china taken from nearby homes. The soldiers had smashed chairs to make kindling for their fires. In one house Bowen found a bacchanalia in progress. One soldier was banging away on a piano, while others sang, danced and guzzled wine. Bowen joined the revelry. Occasionally the Confederates threw a stray shell into the town, but the Union soldiers paid them no heed. "...We were not to be frightened out of our spree," Bowen explained, "for we don't often have one."

E. Porter Alexander

Some soldiers took advantage of the temporary lull in the fighting to write letters home letting family members know that they had survived the bloodshed. A few regiments even received mail, suggesting that postmen of that era not only braved rain and snow in order to make their appointed rounds, but also shot and shell.

The busiest men in the army following the battle were the surgeons. Some 9,600 Union soldiers had been wounded in the fighting, and most of them required immediate care. Those who could walk made their way back across the river to Aquia Creek, where steamships waited to carry them to hospitals in the North. Those with more serious wound made the journey to Aquia Creek via ambulance and train.

The number of Union casualties increased each day that the army remained south of the river. Although there was no general engagement after Dec. 13, opposing artillerymen continued to ply their trade. On the Union side, the firing was slow and deliberate, as if the Northern artillerymen wished to remind Lee that they would not be caught napping should he get it into his mind to attack. On the Confederate side, firing was more sporadic — a round here, a round there, followed by long periods of inactivity. Southern gunners were low on ammunition and had to husband what little remained against the possibility of further attacks.

Skirmishing between opposing infantrymen, by contrast, was unusually active. Although Gen. Burnside had withdrawn his army to Fredericksburg after his defeat, he had left a strong skirmish line in front of Marye's Heights, one half mile outside the town, to keep an eye on the Confederates.

The Union soldiers lay sprawled across an open field on a line that paralleled modern Littlepage Street. They exchanged fire with Confederate riflemen located 150 yards away, in the Sunken Road. The Southerners' fire was particularly spiteful. "We commenced firing at any and every thing moving in our front," remembered one Rebel, "and were wasting so much ammunition and doing so little damage to the enemy that three men from each company only were allowed to shoot. Sometimes we would see a man run from one house to another and we would fire hundreds of shots at him." Union soldiers had to press themselves flat against the earth to avoid the bullets humming just above their heads. "What a sight!" remarked one Northern officer. "To see men by the thousands lying in such a position covered or protected by a slight rise of ground. . . that rise furnishing the only barrier between themselves & death. It fairly made my heart sick."

Yet amid the killing there were instances of courage and compassion. Union skirmishers occupied a tannery near the modern intersection of William and Littlepage streets. From this brick fortress they fired at Confederate artillerymen sheltered behind gun pits on Marye's Heights. (One of these gun pits can be seen today on the Mary Washington College campus, at the northeast corner of William Street and College Avenue.) Lt. Col. E. Porter Alexander of the Confederate army decided to put a halt to their shenanigans. Lowering the muzzle of a cannon, he fired a single shot through the tannery, causing the Union soldiers inside to flee for their lives. As they left the building, Mississippi riflemen mowed them down. One Union soldier, running toward the rear, turned back to help a wounded friend to safety. Southern soldiers raised their rifles to shoot him, but their commander prevented them, declaring, "That man is too brave to be killed." The Confederates instead cheered the courageous man. As he disappeared behind a protective building with his friend, the heroic soldier acknowledged the Confederates' chivalry with a wave of his cap.

South of town things were quieter. In the afternoon, Union and Confederate soldiers called a temporary truce to bury the dead and succor wounded soldiers who had been lying between the lines for 48 hours. By then many of the corpses had become black and bloated. They lay "in every conceivable posture," wrote a witness to the gruesome scene, "some on their backs with gaping jaws, some with eyes as large as walnuts, protruding with glassy stare, some doubled up like a contortionist, here one without a head, there one without legs, yonder a head and legs without a trunk, everywhere horrible expressions, fear, rage, agony, madness, torture, lying in pools of blood, lying with heads half buried in mud, with fragments of shell sticking in oozing brain, with bullet holes all over the puffed limbs...."

Needy Confederates took advantage of the truce to strip the Union dead of their shoes, clothing and weapons. When a Union officer objected to such actions as violating the terms of the cease-fire agreement, a scavenger eyed the man's fine boots and replied, "I'll shoot you tomorrow and git them boots." A short distance away, a Confederate soldier began to remove the shoes from a prostrate Yankee when the man suddenly lifted his head and looked at him in silent reproach. "Beg pardon, sir," the startled Southerner replied, "I thought you had gone above."

While some Confederates took advantage of the truce to scour the field for clothing, others met with their Northern counterparts between the lines to trade newspapers, tobacco and coffee. Watching the soldiers as they chatted and joked together, one would think that they were the best of friends rather than mortal enemies. "It is to[o] bad to make men slaughter each other when they would be friends," wrote a Vermont man, expressing a sentiment shared by thousands that day. The truce lasted only a couple of hours, after which the soldiers returned to their lines and resumed shooting. The killing would not last much longer, however. Even as the two sides talked and traded, Union officers were planning to bring the Army of the Potomac back across the Rappahannock River.

Looking for a friend

The Battle of Fredericksburg

Kirkland Monument on the Fredericksburg battlefield

The Angel of Marye's Heights

On Christmas Day 1862, with the memories of Fredericksburg still fresh in his mind, Gen. Robert E. Lee wrote to his wife lamenting the hardships of war: "What a cruel thing is war: to separate and destroy families and friends, and mar the purest joys and happiness God has granted us in this world; to fill our hearts with hatred instead of love for our neighbors, and to devastate the fair face of this beautiful world."

Yet amid the killing there were individuals whose kindness and compassion lifted the spirit and reminded soldiers of their common humanity. Richard Rowland Kirkland was one such individual. On Dec. 14, 1862, Kirkland risked his life to comfort soldiers who lay wounded in front of Marye's Heights. It is not uncommon for a soldier to risk his life for a friend. What makes Kirkland's story so compelling is that he risked his life to help his enemies.

Kirkland was born in 1843 on his father's farm near Flat Rock, S.C. Like many boys in the rural South, Kirkland grew up learning to shoot rifles and ride horses. An even-tempered, religious lad, he attended Flat Rock Baptist Church and attained a rudimentary education. Kirkland's mother

died when he was just 2 years old, leaving his father to raise five sons and a daughter by himself. Richard was his youngest boy, but he grew up fast. By 1861 he was 5 feet, 8 inches tall and a lithe 150 pounds. A photograph taken of him at this time shows him as having a thin face, brown eyes, dark hair, and a neatly trimmed moustache.

As a young man growing up in the South, Kirkland followed with interest the events leading to the Civil War. On April 9, 1861, he enlisted in Company E of the 2nd South Carolina Volunteers. Three days later, South Carolina forces opened fire on a small United States garrison that had taken refuge inside Fort Sumter, in Charleston harbor, and forced it to surrender. In response, President Abraham Lincoln called upon states loyal to the Union to suppress the rebellion. The war was on.

Kirkland and his comrades initially joined other state troops gathering at Charleston. Later, when Virginia joined the Southern Confederacy, the 2nd South Carolina was sent north to protect the Old Dominion from Northern invasion. The war was still in its infancy then, and anyone in uniform was considered a patriot and a hero. As

Kirkland's regiment moved north, it received an enthusiastic welcome wherever it went. "We was received with [a] warm reception," the proud young soldier wrote his brother from Petersburg, "& glee every where through the state." At each town, citizens welcomed them with food, hugs and flowers. It was heady stuff for a man not yet 19 years of age.

All too soon, however, war's reality set in. In July, Kirkland got his first taste of combat at Bull Run, outside Manassas, Va. Other battles followed: Savage's Station, Malvern Hill, Antietam. Suddenly war did not seem like such a glorious adventure. Kirkland, however, did his duty and did not miss a battle. By December 1862 he was a seasoned veteran.

The 2nd South Carolina Regiment was in the thick of the fighting at Fredericksburg. When Union troops launched their attacks against Marye's Heights on Dec. 13, Gen. Robert E. Lee ordered Gen. Joseph B. Kershaw to reinforce Confederate troops fighting there. Kershaw led the 2nd South Carolina and the other units of his brigade across the plateau and into the Sunken Road below to join regiments from North Carolina and Georgia in repulsing the Union attacks.

The Confederates did their work well: by day's end 1,000 Union soldiers lay dead in front of the Heights. Seven thousand more had been wounded. Unable to move, most of the injured soldiers still lay between the lines when the sun rose the next day. No one could rescue them: to expose oneself on the plain even for an instant meant certain death. "The Yankees were literally piled in our front," remembered one South Carolinian, "dead and dying together, the living crying, water, water!" The cries of one Union soldier were particularly piteous. After calling in vain for his friends to succor him, he cried out: "If my friends

Richard Kirkland succors wounded

cannot give me water, will my enemies give me some?"

Richard Kirkland could not ignore such a plea. As a Christian, he may have remembered the Biblical injunction: "If your enemy is hungry, feed him; if he is thirsty, give him something to drink." Bounding up the stairs of the nearby Stephens house, Kirkland asked Gen. Kershaw for permission to take water to his wounded enemies. Kershaw tried to talk him out of it. "Kirkland, don't you know that you would get a bullet through your head the moment you stepped over the wall?"

"Yes, sir," the young man replied, "I know that; but if you will let me, I am willing to try it." Kershaw could not refuse the noble request. Reluctantly, he gave Kirkland permission to go, trusting that God would protect him. Kirkland hurried back down the stairs, but a moment later he returned. Kershaw assumed the well-intentioned sergeant had had second thoughts, but he was wrong: Kirkland simply wanted to perform his deed under a flag of truce. "General, can I show a white flag?" he inquired. Unfortunately the general could not grant the request. The two sides were locked in combat; only the commanding general could negotiate a truce. Kirkland was undeterred. "All right," he replied, "I'll take the chances."

Borrowing canteens from several friends, Kirkland took a deep breath, jumped over the protective wall bordering the Sunken Road and dashed out onto the deadly plain. Bullets struck the mud around him, but he was not hit. Reaching the nearest soldier, Kirkland knelt down and poured the cooling liquid down the man's throat. He then took the soldier's knapsack and placed it under his head for a pillow at the same time laying the man's overcoat across him for a blanket.

By now, the Union

riflemen understood Kirkland's mission and had ceased firing at him. Some even cheered his bravery. For the next 90 minutes Kirkland moved slowly about the field, giving aid to all he could reach. Who knows how many men benefited from his mercy?

As a result of his actions, Kirkland became known as "The Angel of Marye's Heights." He died just nine months later at the Battle of Chickamauga, but his deed at Fredericksburg was not forgotten. In 1965, local citizens led by Dr. Richard Nunn Lanier petitioned the state legislatures of Virginia and South Carolina to construct a monument to Kirkland's memory. Today it stands at the northeast corner of Mercer Street and Sunken Road, a rare testimony to man's humanity to man.

Richard R. Kirkland

Retreat from Fredericksburg

The Union Army Retreats

On the night of Dec. 14, 1862, an unearthly ribbon of light illuminated the sky above Fredericksburg: an aurora borealis. Although it lasted just 30 minutes, this rare spectacle was seen by the Confederates as an omen of triumph, as if "the heavens were hanging out banners and streamers and setting off fireworks in honor of our victory."

To the mind of Robert E. Lee and most other soldiers on the field, the battle was not over. The Union army had been defeated the previous day — and soundly — but it had not been crushed. Lee fully expected his opponent, Gen. Ambrose E. Burnside, to renew the attacks he had begun on Dec. 13. Once Burnside had again bloodied his army against the Confederates' impenetrable defenses, Lee would go over to the offensive and drive the Northern army into the Rappahannock River. But he would not get that chance. Burnside's officers persuaded him that further attacks would be useless, and the Union commander reluctantly ordered the army to retreat back across the Rappahannock on the night of Dec. 15.

Luck was with Burnside that night. After dark a storm blew in hard from the west, obscuring the moon and blowing the sound of the retreat away from the Confederates on the hills outside of town. On the heels of this gale came a torrential rain that added to night's intense darkness. All this worked to Burnside's advantage, for it prevented Lee from detecting the retreat. Had he done so, Lee could have attacked the Union army as it lay straddled across the river and perhaps destroyed it. As it was, the Union army escaped. "Perhaps in a whole year so good a night for that purpose could not be had again," thought one Union staff officer.

Burnside began sending ambulances and supply wagons across the river during the day. As darkness set in, cavalry, artillery, and infantry joined the procession. To muffle the sound of the Union army as it crossed the river, soldiers scattered dirt, pine branches, sawdust, and other debris across the wooden pontoon bridges. Straw wrapped around the wheels of wagons and cannon also helped dampen the sound. Soldiers spoke in whispered voices and tied down their tin cups to prevent them from rattling as they walked. Any noise that could give the army away was strictly forbidden. Its safety, indeed its very existence, depended on secrecy and silence.

South of town, near the modern Fredericksburg Country Club, Gen. William B. Franklin quietly began pulling his troops out of line and sending them toward pontoon bridges in the rear. An informal truce between the opposing pickets aided Franklin in his task. By 4 a.m., his entire grand division — 40,000 men — was safely across the Rappahannock and marching toward its old camps near White Oak Church.

Farther north, in front of Marye's Heights, there was no truce, making it more difficult for the Union army to slip away. Confederate pickets had advanced 75 yards in front of the stone wall that bordered the sunken road, placing them well within earshot of Union soldiers, who were just a stone's throw away. Col. Edward Hill's 16th Michigan was one of several Union regiments sent to picket front the that night. Advancing out Hanover Street toward Marye's Heights, it crossed the millrace (now Kenmore Avenue), angled left, and climbed the bluff beyond. At the top of the hill, the regiment encountered a line of men lying on their weapons. When Hill inquired as to their corps, the men did not respond. They were dead, victims of the Dec. 13 fighting. Under the cover of darkness someone had laid out their corpses in a row to imitate a line of battle. "The stern necessities of war," Hill grimly observed, were "still exacting duty from the dead."

While Hill's regiment and others kept their sleepless vigil in front of Marye's Heights, Union soldiers in town quietly made their way back across the river. It was after 3 a.m. before many of the pickets learned that the army had retreated. "Imagine our feelings," wrote Nathaniel Brown of the 133rd Pennsylvania. "Here we were, within 200 yards of the rebel batteries, and the majority

of the army already across the river. What if the enemy should become aware of this...and fall upon us? Few of us would escape." Only after the rest of the army was safely across were the pickets allowed to fall back. One by one, the men crept back through the deserted town and hurried toward the river. Occasionally the moon would break through the clouds, casting light on the corpses that littered the streets. "The flicker of that light, the loud moaning of the wind, and the rattling of shattered houses...made a feeling of dread creep over one — which was not easily banished," wrote Brown. "There is something, certainly not courage breeding, in such a night and amid such scenes."

Lt. Col. Joshua Chamberlain would have agreed. Chamberlain and his 20th Maine Volunteers were also on picket duty that night. The first knowledge they had that the army was retreating was when a staff officer galloped up in the darkness and said in an excited voice, "Get yourselves out of this as quick as God will let you! The whole army is across the river!" Chamberlain quickly had his men count off by twos. While half the soldiers dug in as loudly as possible to deceive the enemy, Chamberlain led the other half back to a point 100 yards to the rear. Once they were in place, those at the front quietly left their position and fell back to a point 100 yards behind the second line. Chamberlain continued the leapfrogging process until his men were well away from the Confederate line, then hurried them toward the bridges. Southern pickets fired a stray shot or two in their direction. At the same time, a dog let out a mournful howl "as if he too were set upon our tracks." Chamberlain's men picked up their pace.

Meanwhile, back at the river, Union engineers waited impatiently for the last regiments to arrive before taking up their bridges. One floating span remained in place until 8:30 a.m. By then, the Confederates had discovered the retreat and were cautiously entering the town. Rather than take time to dismantle the bridge, engineers simply cut loose the southern end and allowed the current to push it over to the Stafford shore. Officers later sent pontoon boats back across the

Burnside issues orders to retreat

river to pick up stragglers who had lagged behind. Even so, several hundred prisoners fell into Confederate hands.

By 9 a.m., the crossing was complete. Without exception, it was hailed as a great accomplishment. "We had not expected to get away so cheaply," wrote a soldier in the 35th New York. "To move an army with a six mile front, every foot of which was menaced by the enemy's lines at a distance of twenty to fifty rods, and withdraw the pickets without discovery, was no small undertaking." Artilleryman George Breck agreed. "...The retreat began and was conducted from beginning to end almost noiselessly, without a particle of panic.... The pontoon bridges were taken up, and scarcely a thing was left behind." If the Army of the Potomac had done nothing else right in the campaign, its retreat at least had been a success. The army would live to fight another day.

Burying the dead

Burying the Dead

The Battle of Fredericksburg was over. The smoking rifles and belching cannons had fallen silent. The Union army was gone. Yet evidence of the fighting remained in the form of battered houses, scarred landscapes, and decomposing bodies. More than 1,700 soldiers had been killed in the battle. Many of the corpses had been left behind, unburied, in the Army of the Potomac's retreat. Gen. Robert E. Lee of the Confederate army attended to the burial of his own dead and sent a message to his Union counterpart, Gen. Ambrose E. Burnside, requesting that Burnside send detachments back across the Rappahannock River to inter the Northern dead. The Union commander readily assented to the proposal.

Gen. Edwin Sumner detailed three officers and 100 men from the Second and Ninth corps for the task. Soldiers from other corps also may have taken part. Col. John R. Brooke of the 53rd Pennsylvania led the Second Corps detachment. The Union army had interred most of the soldiers who had died in the fighting south of Fredericksburg during a flag of truce on Dec. 15, 1862, so the burial parties focused on Marye's Heights sector of the battlefield, directly behind the town.

Brooke and his men crossed the Rappahannock River below the Lacy House (Chatham) early on Dec. 17 and were escorted by a detail of Confederate soldiers from the 13th Mississippi Regiment to the plain outside of town. "As we approached the battle field," wrote one soldier, "the sight reminded me of a flock of sheep reposing in the field. But as we approached nearer, who can describe my feelings when I found them to be the dead bodies of our brave men, which had been stripped of their clothing." Confederate soldiers, lacking sufficient uniforms, had stolen the coats, pants and even the undergarments of their fallen foe as protection against the coming winter.

Once they reached the plain the Union burial party fanned out and began gathering up the corpses for burial. It was a gruesome task. "They were literally pieces of men, for those destructive shells had done their perfect work," wrote one soldier. "It was the worst sight I ever beheld, and may I be spared another such a scene." While some of the soldiers gathered in the battle's harvest, other fashioned a ditch, approximately 6 feet wide and 100 yards long, from a defensive trench started by Union soldiers during the battle. The trench began at Hanover Street and extended south in a line just east of modern-day Littlepage

Headless corpse sitting on a litter

Street. As soldiers brought the bodies in, they laid them side-by-side in the ditch, three deep, and covered them with a thin layer of dirt.

In all, 609 men were buried there. Among them was the owner of a Newfoundland dog. For two days and nights, the faithful animal had kept vigil beside his master's lifeless corpse. Now, as strangers tossed dirt over the soldier's mortal remains, the dog showed an almost "human sympathy, more so," thought one observer "than any there in human shape."

The work was not completed by day's end, prompting Gen. Burnside to request a second flag of truce on Dec. 18. Lee granted the request and once again Union soldiers, 200 to 300 in number, rowed across the Rappahannock River into Fredericksburg. On the other side a body of Mississippi troops dressed in ragged garments and carrying a white flag met them. The Southerners greeted the party in a friendly manner, shaking hands with them and asking them questions about the recent battle. Some swapped small trinkets — a stamp, for instance, or a piece of hardtack.

As they had the day before, the Confederates led the burial party through Fredericksburg to the plain in front of Marye's Heights. The destruction in town was immense. "Fredericksburg is knocked all to pieces," wrote one soldier. "Every house almost is full of holes where the shells have been

sent. Possibly it may be repaired again but I think [it] doubtful." Dead horses littered the streets, their carcasses lying amid smashed furniture, broken crockery, and trampled clothes. Using boards for stretchers, the soldiers again fanned out to look for bodies. Some corpses had been in the sun for five days and had turned black. "Oh it was awful!" wrote one nauseated worker. "All of them were struck either in the head or breast mostly with musket balls. Those shot in the head were hit in the forehead eyes mouth, everywhere in the head." They placed 23 bodies in one ditch and 125 in another. 'We laid the poor fellows side by side in the trench & covered them with earth where they will remain till the great Judgement Day. O! What a dreadful war this is!"

As the burial party carried out its solemn task, Confederate soldiers casually looked on. Some of them taunted the Federals by holding up blue clothing that had been stripped from the dead, asserting that they would continue to fight as long as the Yankees occupied their soil. Confederate Gens. William Barksdale, Lafayette McLaws, and J.E.B. Stuart stopped by during the day to look in on the work. Also present was Maj. Heros von Borcke, a huge Prussian officer serving on Stuart's staff. Von Borcke was shocked at the rough manner in which the Union soldiers handled their dead. On the battlefield was an icehouse with a deep pit. As Von Borcke looked on, Northern soldiers tossed corpses into the hole "until the solid mass of human flesh reached near the surface, when a covering of logs, chalk, and mud closed the mouth of this vast and awful tomb."

To the Prussian officer it seemed as if the Federals were more interested in doing the job quickly than in doing it well. Nor was he alone in that opinion. Nearby, Union soldiers opened a second trench and hastily filled it with 130 bodies. A Fredericksburg citizen, Edward Heinichen, noted the shallowness of the graves. The bodies received such a superficial burial, he complained, "that parts of them after a short time showed above ground, & dogs brought home many a limb. Some corpses were entirely overlooked, & I recollect to have seen two of them untouched as late as the following April."

At the end of the truce period, the Union soldiers shouldered their tools and started back. With them they brought the bodies of five officers found on the field. A woman whose home had been destroyed during the battle followed the Federals as they returned to town, hurling "the most wrathful imprecations" at the Yankee invaders. She followed the party all the way to the riverbank, crying out that she wished they too were dead. More gracious were the farewells of the Mississippians who bid their foes good-bye "in the most friendly manner." Reflecting on his interactions with the Rebel escort, a Union soldier concluded, "What a pity that we must fight."

The next day Col. Brooke drafted a report of the expedition. He recorded burying a total of 913 bodies, not counting the five that he had brought back across the river. The job, however, had not been done well. As Edward Heinichen noted, the bodies had been buried in shallow graves, and after heavy rains the bones rose to the surface. News of the poor burial conditions got back to officials in Washington. When the war ended in July 1865, the War Department established Fredericksburg National Cemetery on Marye's Heights. Over the next three years, contract workers collected the remains of 15,000 Union soldiers from battlefields throughout central Virginia and brought them to Fredericksburg for burial. (Confederate soldiers who died in the area were buried at private expense in two local cemeteries.) By then, however, most identification had disappeared. As a result, just 16 percent of the soldiers now buried in the cemetery have been identified.

The War Department administered Fredericksburg National Cemetery until 1933, when it transferred the property to the National Park Service. It is open daily from dawn until dusk.

Fredericksburg National Cemetery

Ambrose Burnside Bows Out

The Fredericksburg Campaign began on Nov. 7, 1862, when Gen. Ambrose E. Burnside received orders to take command of the Army of the Potomac. It ended 11 weeks later on Jan. 26, 1863, when, at the orders of President Abraham Lincoln, Burnside turned command of the army over to Gen. Joseph Hooker. The president had a high personal regard for Burnside, but he realized that the general had the confidence of neither the army nor its officers. The main reason for that, of course, was Burnside's defeat at Fredericksburg. The Army of the Potomac had suffered defeat before, but never had it been so decisive and so obvious. Everyone in the army, from generals down to privates, knew that the attacks against Marye's Heights could not succeed, and yet Burnside had insisted on making them. As a result, the army had been slaughtered and very nearly annihilated. "What a bloody, one-sided battle this was," complained one soldier. "It was simply murder, and the whole army is mad about it. We are no fools! We can see when we have a chance; here we had none." It was not simply that Union soldiers had suffered, but rather that their suffering had been to no purpose. The army, noted one reporter, was "decimated and despondent, the soldiers feeling deeply, more acutely than words can tell, that they were dying in vain."

Sullenness pervaded the ranks. The troops were dissatisfied with everyone and everything. They had lost faith in the government, in their commanders, and in themselves. "There is a feeling of deep and painful anxiety as to the future," Gen. Marsena Patrick confided in his journal. "No confidence is felt in any one." Demoralization frequently boiled over into anger, the soldiers lashing out at any and everybody whom they held responsible for the disaster. William F. Morgan of the 2nd Massachusetts Volunteers thought that "The slaughter at Fredericksburg is a disgrace to the world, and there should be a Hell made expressly for its authors. To concentrate an army in an open field exposed to two cross fires...is an idea so preposterous that no one but a fool or a lunatic would ever conceive." Robert Pratt of the 5th Vermont was even more severe in his denunciations. "I am yet alive in this wicked war," he informed his family. "A war carried on and thousands after thousands of men being killed and made crippled for life. And for what, god only knows.... For army controllers and for a mess of men that were damn fools trying to make themselves eminent men in the eyes of the people by lives of others. But it is most played out.... I shall never fight any more. I think I can say with out lying that [I] have done my duty well since [I] enlisted. But now to go and be murdered for nothing...I shall not. Terrible is the punishment of this nation."

Blame for the disaster fell squarely on the army's commander. "...Almost everyone was cursing Burnside as the author of the defeat at Fredericksburg," wrote John B. Vance of Pennsylvania. "At the Reviews when he rode along the lines & the Col[onel]s would call out — 'Three cheers for Burnside' the men would stand silent & sullen or mutter curses against him." Even those who personally liked Burnside felt he was not up the job. "Burnsides [sic] may be a good enough man but he is not the man to command such an army as the Army of the Potomac," wrote one soldier.

The lack of confidence in Burnside's ability pervaded all levels of the army. Gen. William B. Franklin confided after Fredericksburg that he had "lost all confidence" in Burnside's ability. "There was not a man in my command who did not believe that everything he would undertake would fail," he asserted.

Burnside wrote a public letter manfully shouldering full responsibility for the disaster, but that only lowered him in some men's eyes. "What an awful greenhorn Burnside is, don't you think so too?" Lt. Henry Abbott wrote to his family in Boston. "His letter is the letter of a high-minded donkey, if it is high-minded at all, which I am beginning to doubt...." Even those who admired Burnside's courage in taking responsibility for the loss felt that he had to go. "His assumption of all blame for the defeat is worthy of him," wrote a

soldier in the 118th Pennsylvania Volunteers. "But it will not atone for the slaughter of so many brave men."

The debacle at Fredericksburg convinced many Union soldiers that prosecution of the war was fruitless. Maj. Franklin Pierce of the 108th New York admitted that "the whole army is disheartened and discouraged and it is certain that by arms the [Southern Confederacy] can never be subdued." Lt. Abbott blamed the army's defeat on politicians in the nation's capital. "The strongest peace party is the army," he declared. "If the small fry at Washington want to hear treason talked, let them come to the army.... I firmly believe that...the men who ordered the crossing of the river are responsible to God for murder. How long you people at home are going to stand it I don't know, but if we again have to turn our backs on the rebel enemy, we shan't stop untill [sic] we get to Washington & lay our hands on our true enemies, those blood stained scoundrels in the government."

The army was in a dangerous, surly mood. Only victory would revive it. In an effort to restore the army's confidence, Burnside planned a surprise crossing of the Rappahannock River below Fredericksburg on New Year's Day 1863. At

COLUMBIA. "Where are my 15,000 Sons—murdered at Fredericksburg?"   LINCOLN. "This reminds me of a little Joke—"   COLUMBIA. "Go tell your Joke AT SPRINGFIELD!!"

An editorial cartoon critical of Lincoln from *Harper's Weekly*, Jan. 3, 1863 the same time, Union cavalry would cross the Rappahannock at Kelly's Ford, 20 miles above the town, and strike south destroying railroads, bridges and canals. Two of Burnside's officers alerted President Lincoln to the plan, however, and warned him that it would lead to disaster. Alarmed by this message, Lincoln wired Burnside ordering him to make no forward movement without first consulting him. When the general learned that two of his officers had gone behind his back to subvert his plan, he was livid. He demanded that the president expose the two informers, but Lincoln refused to do so. Burnside had his sources, however, and he soon discovered the culprits' identities.

Meanwhile, the general revived his plans for a midwinter offensive. This time, instead of crossing the Rappahannock down river from Fredericksburg, he planned to move upstream and cross at Banks' Ford. (Banks' Ford is located near the spot where River Road grazes the Rappahannock River in Spotsylvania County, less than a mile west of Bragg Road.) The movement got underway on Jan. 20, 1863. The weather was unusually mild. In the evening the winds shifted, however, and by 7 p.m. it began to rain. For two days it poured steadily, saturating the countryside and turning the unpaved roads into knee-deep mud. Burnside's luck had failed him again. After struggling for two days in the bottomless mire, the Union general reluctantly ordered his troops back to camp. The Mud March was over.

In the wake of this episode, the army's discontent reached new heights. Soldiers began deserting by the hundreds, then by the thousands. "The Army of the Potomac is no more an army," declared one officer. "Its patriotism has oozed out through the pores opened by the imbecility of its leaders, and the fatigues and disappointments of a fruitless campaign." Army officers spoke openly of their contempt for Burnside's leadership. Leading the chorus of criticism was Gen. Joseph Hooker, Burnside's chief rival.

Burnside could not command the army effectively under such circumstances and determined to clean house. On Jan. 23, he drafted General Order No. 8, dismissing or relieving from duty nine of the army's top officers. Joe Hooker's name headed the list. Before taking action, however, Burnside first showed the order to President Lincoln. The order would create quite a stir in military and political circles, and Burnside wanted to make sure that he had the president's support. If Lincoln refused to approve the order, Burnside would offer his resignation. One way or the other, things would change.

Lincoln liked Burnside, but it was obvious to him that the general no longer possessed the confidence of the army. After discussing General Order No. 8 with members of his cabinet, the president relieved Burnside of command and appointed Joe Hooker to take his place. The Fredericksburg Campaign — the darkest chapter in the Army of the Potomac's history — was over.

President William McKinley in Fredericksburg, 1900

The Battlefield Becomes a Park

By the time the Civil War ended in 1865, Fredericksburg was in ruins. The once elegant town had been shattered by artillery fire, pillaged by enemy soldiers, and turned into one vast hospital. Its citizens had fled; its economy was in tatters. But Fredericksburg rebounded. After the war approximately 4,000 of the town's 5,000 inhabitants returned. In time they restored their shell-torn houses, reopened their factories and shops, and rebuilt their lives.

In 1866, construction began on a national cemetery located at Marye's Heights, just outside of town. Over the next three years, civilian contractors hired by the United States government combed the lots, fields and forests around Fredericksburg, hunting for Union graves. The bodies, when found, were brought to the cemetery by wagon and buried. The bodies of Southern soldiers were taken to Confederate cemeteries located either in Fredericksburg or at Spotsylvania Court House. Over time, granite headstones replaced wooden markers over the graves, and monuments graced the grounds. Northern and Southern cemeteries alike began to take on a permanent look.

Rancor engendered by the war steadily subsided, and by 1890 Union and Confederate veterans were working together to preserve the battlefields where they once had fought. Sites of Northern victories received top priority. Antietam, Chickamauga and Chattanooga, Shiloh, Gettysburg and Vicksburg battlefields became national military parks in the 1890s. The Fredericksburg-area battlefields, being mostly Confederate victories, received less attention.

Even so, there were those who were determined to see the land preserved. In 1891, a group of veterans formed a corporation for the purpose of creating a national military park at Fredericksburg. The group got off to a fast start, purchasing 747 acres at Spotsylvania Court House Battlefield and 845 acres at Chancellorsville. Unfortunately, it was unable to pay its bills, and the land reverted to private ownership in 1895.

Aspirations for a national military park at Fredericksburg lived on, however. In 1898, at the prompting of the Fredericksburg City Council, the Virginia Assembly passed legislation creating the Fredericksburg National Park Commission. It appointed prominent veterans such as Joshua Chamberlain, Dan Sickles and James Longstreet to serve on its executive committee. The commission's goal was "to mark and preserve the battlefields" around Fredericksburg and to erect "memorial stones, tablets or monuments" as needed. It had the authority to purchase up to 7,125 acres of land that could be transferred later to the United States government to create a national military park.

Two years later, in May 1900, the Society of the Army of the Potomac, one of the largest Union veterans' groups in the country, held its annual reunion at Fredericksburg. It was the first time the society had held a meeting in the South, and it attracted national attention. President William McKinley, himself an old soldier, attended the meeting, as did the governor of Virginia and numerous generals. Judge John T. Goolrick welcomed the group on behalf of the city. Addressing the crowd of former officers and dignitaries, the former Confederate private quipped that he was the most distinguished man present at the gathering, being one of the few enlisted men there. Before leaving Fredericksburg members of the society sent a resolution to the United States Congress supporting the creation of a national park at Fredericksburg. The Speaker of the House op-

posed the measure, however, and blocked its passage. Despite the best efforts of the Fredericksburg National Park Commission and its allies, the bill never reached the House floor.

For 20 years the idea of a national military park at Fredericksburg languished. It revived in 1921 when Gen. Smedley Butler brought 4,200 Marines from Quantico to Wilderness Battlefield for four days of military exercises. The Marines sketched the outline of a battleship in the valley bordering Wilderness Run (near the present-day intersection of Routes 3 and 20) and for four days defended the ship against mock assaults from the air. The exercise, which was attended by President Warren G. Harding and Marine Commandant Maj. Gen. John A. Lejeune, attracted national attention and provided new impetus to create a national military park at Fredericksburg.

That dream finally became a reality in 1927, when Congress passed a bill establishing Fredericksburg and Spotsylvania County Battlefields Memorial National Military Park. The new park encompassed four major Civil War battlefields — Fredericksburg, Chancellorsville, Wilderness and Spotsylvania Court House — on which 100,000 soldiers had been killed, wounded or captured. President Calvin Coolidge formally dedicated the park in 1928 at a ceremony held at the Fredericksburg Country Club, south of town. Virginia's governor, Harry Byrd, and Sen. Claude

President Warren G. Harding, Gen. Smedley Butler and Judge John T. Goolrick

The Battle of Fredericksburg

A. Swanson attended the ceremony.

Development of the park proceeded at a fast pace. Park commissioners purchased more than 2,100 acres of ground and in 1931 opened Lee Drive, the park's first tour road. Then the Great Depression hit. Work ground to a halt as funding for the park dried up. But the Depression turned out to be a blessing in disguise. In 1933, President Franklin D. Roosevelt transferred Fredericksburg National Military Park from the War Department to the National Park Service and infused money into it through various New Deal programs. Progress in developing the park jumped forward. The Civilian Conservation Corps constructed roads, built culverts, and cleared trees off of trenches; the Public Works Administration constructed a visitor center at the corner of Lafayette Boulevard and Sunken Road; Emergency Conservation Work guides manned contact stations and squired visitors around the park. As a result of these projects, Fredericksburg battlefield began taking on the look of a modern national park.

Land acquisitions since then have helped fill out the park boundaries. In 1975 philanthropist John Lee Pratt donated his 18th-century home, Chatham, to the park, and in 1997 the National Park Service, with financial assistance from the Civil War Preservation Trust (CWPT) and the Central Virginia Battlefield Trust (CVBT), purchased a key portion of Marye's Heights adjacent to Fredericksburg National Cemetery.

At the time of this writing (2002) the Na-

Coolidge Monument

tional Park Service is working to acquire lots along Willis Street in an effort to restore a small portion of the plain leading to Marye's Heights — hallowed ground on which more than 1,000 Union soldiers lost their lives. Thanks to the efforts of the Fredericksburg City Council, several hundred yards of the historic Sunken Road — the site of two major battles — will soon be closed to traffic and restored to its historic appearance.

Other exciting projects are in the works: new films for the visitor center, new outdoor exhibits along the Sunken Road and Marye's Heights, a new audio walking tour. In conjunction with the City of Fredericksburg and partners like the CVBT, the National Park Service is also working to interpret Civil War sites outside the park boundary. Sign clusters at the city dock, the Education Board Building, Maury School, and the Fredericksburg City Visitor Center attest to the success of these partnerships.

Today, at approximately 8,000 acres, Fredericksburg and Spotsylvania County National Military Park is the largest military reservation in the world. Nearly 80,000 people come to Fredericksburg each year to visit Marye's Heights, to walk the Sunken Road, and to learn about the tragic events that took place there. They come to reflect and to remember. That is what the veterans who fought to establish the park more than a century ago intended. They would be pleased to know that it had finally come to pass.

A Selected Annotated Bibliography

Brainerd, Wesley. *Bridge Building in Wartime: Col. Wesley Brainerd's Memoir of the 50th New York Volunteer Engineers.* Edited by Ed Malles. (Knoxville: The University of Tennessee Press, 1997). Brainerd was an engineering officer charged with constructing one of the six pontoon bridges across the Rappahannock River. This account of his wartime services is among the most interesting and skillfully written narratives of the war.

Catton, Bruce. *Glory Road: The Bloody Route from Fredericksburg to Gettysburg,* (Garden City, New York: Doubleday & Company, Inc., 1952). The second volume in a trilogy about the Army of the Potomac, written by the Civil War's most celebrated author.

Freeman, Douglas S. *Lee's Lieutenants. The Study of the Army of Northern Virginia and Its Leaders,* 3 vols. (New York: Charles Scribner's Sons, 1944). Although written more than half a century ago, this three-volume series remains a military classic.

Gallagher, Gary W., ed. *The Fredericksburg Campaign: Decision on the Rappahannock,* (Chapel Hill: The University of North Carolina Press, 1995). A fine series of essays written by leading historians including Robert K. Krick, Alan Nolan and Carol Reardon.

Goolrick, William K. *Rebels Resurgent: Fredericksburg to Chancellorsville,* (Alexandria, Virginia: Time-Life Books, 1985). This short, well-illustrated history of Fredericksburg and Chancellorsville is part of Time-Life Corporation's series on Civil War battles.

Harrison, Noel G. *Fredericksburg Battlefield Sites,* Volume Two, December 1862-April 1865. (Lynchburg, Virginia: H.E. Howard, Inc., 1995). A guide to houses and other structures that played a role in the campaign. Packed with useful information but not geared toward the casual reader.

Johnson, Robert U. and Clarence C. Buel, eds. *Battles and Leaders of the Civil War.* 4 vols. (New York: The Century Company, 1884-1888). A compendium of articles about the war written by participants.

Luvaas, Jay, and Harold W. Nelson, eds. *The U.S. Army War College Guide to the Battles of Chancellorsville and Fredericksburg,* (New York: Harper & Rowe Publishers, 1988). A site-specific battlefield guide written to facilitate military staff rides. Relies heavily on after-action reports submitted by the combatants.

Marvel, William. *The Battle of Fredericksburg,* (Philadelphia: Eastern National, 1993). A short, affordable narrative of the battle, perfect for Civil War novices. Fine maps and illustrations.

Mathless, Paul, ed., *Voices of the Civil War: Fredericksburg.* (Alexandria, Virginia: Time-Life Books, 1997). An outstanding compilation of battle accounts, written by the soldiers themselves. Superior illustrations and maps.

McCarter, William. *My Life in the Irish Brigade: The Civil War Memoirs of Private William McCarter, 116th Pennsylvania Infantry.* Edited by Kevin E. O'Brien. (Campbell, California: Savas Publishing Co., 1996). McCarter's detailed account of his sufferings is among the best written by any soldier, North or South.

O'Reilly, Francis A. *The Fredericksburg Campaign: Winter War on the Rappahannock.* (Baton Rouge, Louisiana: Louisiana State University Press, 2003). The single best book on the military aspects of the battle. Well researched and skillfully written.

Rable, George C. *Fredericksburg! Fredericksburg!* (Chapel Hill: University of North Carolina Press, 2002).

A fine, full-length study of Fredericksburg. Utilizes a wide array of previously untapped sources.

Savas, Theordore P., and Daniel A. Woodbury. *Blood on the Rappahannock: The Battle of Fredericksburg*, in the series *Civil War Regiments: A Journal of the Civil War*, vol. 4, no. 4 (Campbell, California: Regimental Studies, Inc., 1995). A series of excellent essays covering different facets of the battle ranging from the death of Gen. Thomas Cobb to the street fighting experienced by the 20th Massachusetts Volunteers.

Stackpole, Edward J. *Drama on the Rappahannock: The Fredericksburg Campaign*, (Harrisburg: The Stackpole Company, 1957). The first full-length history of the campaign. Excellent maps and graphics compensate for a weak, and often biased, text.

Sutherland, Daniel E. *Fredericksburg and Chancellorsville: The Dare Mark Campaign*, (Lincoln: University of Nebraska Press, 1998). A concise, readable history of Fredericksburg and Chancellorsville, which the author views as a single campaign.

Whan, Vorin E., Jr. *Fiasco at Fredericksburg*, (State College, Pennsylvania: The Pennsylvania State University Press, 1961). A short, analytical study of the battle. Instructive but dry.

Illustration Sources

Cumberland County, New Jersey, Historical Society: 96.

Edward J. Stackpole, *Drama on the Rappahannock: The Fredericksburg Campaign*, (Harrisburg: The Stackpole Company, 1957): 18, 21, 44, 109, 110.

Edwin Forbes, *Army Sketch Book: Thirty Years After, an Artist's Story of the Great War*, (New York: Fords, Howard & Hulbert, 1890): 30, 112.

Francis Trevelyan Miller, *The Photographic History of the Civil War*, 10 vols. (New York: The Review of Reviews Co., 1912): 19, 83.

Frank Leslie's Illustrated Newspaper: 91.

Fredericksburg and Spotsylvania County Battlefields Memorial National Military Park: 14, 20, 24, 34, 42, 53, 54, 57, 58, 63, 69, 72, 73, 103, 104, 111, 117.

Gettysburg National Military Park: 41, 43.

Harper's Weekly: 113.

James Longstreet, *From Manassas to Appomattox: Memoirs of the Civil War in America, by James Longstreet, Lieutenant-General Confederate Army*, (Philadelphia: J. B. Lippincott Co., 1896): 79.

John Esten Cooke, *Stonewall Jackson: A Military Biography*, (New York: D. Appleton and Company, 1876): 80.

John T. Goolrick, *Historic Fredericksburg: The Story of an Old Town*, (Richmond: Whittet & Shepperson, 1922): 116.

Larry Massie Collection: 39, 40.

Library of Congress, Washington, D.C.: 15, 20, 22, 29, 32, 37, 46, 47, 49, 50, 52, 55, 65, 70, 74, 75, 76, 77, 81, 85, 87, 89, 93, 94, 101, 108, 113.

Mrs. F. Byrd Holloway Collection: 115.

National Archives, Washington, D.C.: 16, 23, 56, 71, 78, 88, 95, 96.

Robert Underwood Johnson and Clarence Clough Buel, eds., *Battles and Leaders of the Civil War*, 4 vols. (New York: The Century Co., 1884-1887): 27, 31, 33, 35, 36, 38, 51, 59, 60, 61, 62, 64, 66, 67, 68, 90, 100, 102, 106.

South Caroliniana Library, University of South Carolina: 105.

The Illustrated London News: 26.

United States Army Military History Institute, Carlisle Barracks, Pennsylvania: 25, 82, 97, 98.

Valentine Richmond History Center: 54, 84.

Warren Lee Goss, *Recollections of a Private*, (New York: Thomas Y. Crowell & Co., 1890): 13.